RELIGIOUS VOCATION
AN UNNECESSARY MYSTERY

"And every one that hath left house, or brethren, or sisters, or father, or mother, or wife, or children, or lands for my name's sake, shall receive a hundredfold, and shall possess life everlasting." —Matthew 19:29

RELIGIOUS VOCATION
AN UNNECESSARY MYSTERY

By
Fr. Richard Butler, O.P.
DOCTOR OF PHILOSOPHY,
LECTOR OF SACRED THEOLOGY

Foreword by
Most Rev. Edwin Vincent Byrne, D.D.
ARCHBISHOP OF SANTA FE

> *"Jesus saith to him: If thou wilt be perfect, go sell what thou hast, and give to the poor, and thou shalt have treasure in heaven: and come follow me."*
> —Matthew 19:21

TAN BOOKS AND PUBLISHERS, INC.
Rockford, Illinois 61105

REVISORES ORDINIS: Justin Aldridge, O.P.
                      J. S. Reidy, O.P.

IMPRIMI POTEST: Edmund Marr, O.P., S.T.M.
                      Provincial

NIHIL OBSTAT: J. S. Reidy, O.P.
                      Censor Deputatus

IMPRIMATUR: ✚ Albert Cardinal Meyer, S.T.D., S.S.L.
                      Archbishop of Chicago
                      December 5, 1960

Reprinted in 2005 by TAN Books and Publishers, Inc.

ISBN 0-89555-823-8

Image on cover: A detail of "The Dominican Blessed," by Fra Angelico (d. 1455), from the predella (lower section) of the high altarpiece of San Domenico at Fiesole, near Florence. This was the church of Fra Angelico's Dominican friary. Photo © National Gallery, London.

Cover design by Sebrina Higdon.

Printed and bound in the United States of America.

TAN BOOKS AND PUBLISHERS, INC.
P. O. Box 424
Rockford, Illinois 61105
2005

Sincerely dedicated to
Father Gilbert James Graham, O.P.,
Director of Vocations for the Dominican Province
of St. Albert the Great,
who has for many years and with much success put
into practice the principles which I now put into print.

With gratitude to
Archbishop Byrne for
his introduction to this book;
to Father Stephen Reidy, O.P.,
and Father Justin Aldridge, O.P.,
of the Dominican House of Studies,
for reading and criticizing the manuscript;
to Jane Mims and Betty Drake
for typing the final drafts.

—THE AUTHOR

CONTENTS

FOREWORD

To be invited to write a foreword to a work of such stature and dignity as this present volume of Father Richard Butler, O.P., is both a pleasure and a privilege. Our enthusiastic commendation of Father Butler's achievement in these pages will, we are sure, be shared by all who read and ponder his words with the meditative deliberation they deserve.

This is a book for those souls who, in the words of the author, "dare to undertake great things for God." As we may expect from a priest of Father Butler's academic background and apostolic experience, the message of this beautiful work is alive with the throbbing drama of a divine adventure in love. Here we will hear, with clarity and vision, a basic restatement of God's invitation to generous spirits who have entered into that search for perfection we have come to call "the religious life."

Probing deftly into the central significance of the Divine Call in the soul's progress towards eternal glory, the author presents a finely reasoned analysis of the workings of God's grace in the human heart. There is no room for merely sentimental or subjective piety in our study of the interior structure of a religious vocation; the eternal destiny of a particular soul is always involved, and we can ill afford to toy with illusory psychological hypotheses. We welcome, therefore, the publication of this book, in our consideration a unique contribution to the literature of the vocational apostolate.

More than a manual for harried Vocation Directors, however, this work provides illuminating answers to some vexing questions posed by the more mature student in his effort to ascertain the Divine Will in his life. At almost every turn, there arise those who would "promote vocations" at apparently any cost; the result is an inevitable confusion, even an aura of unnecessary mystery, about the true realities of the religious state. Some would wreathe a religious vocation in the remote abstractions of a mysterious inner inspiration. Others popularize the ideals of a religious profession to levels dangerously close to stylized Hollywood glamor. Father Butler, in traditional Thomistic fashion, sets his theme firmly on the middle way towards the truth of the matter in all its wondrous beauty.

And the truth, of course, possesses this beauty because of its divine simplicity. Controversies have raged over religious vocations for centuries; divergent points of view have competed vigorously for popular acceptance. In the eye of our semantic hurricanes, the truth holds fast: Christ has touched the hearts of men and women in the world with the repeated urging to follow Him more closely through the Evangelical Counsels as fulfilled in the religious vows of poverty, chastity, and obedience. This prompting of love is a profoundly personal experience, an inner drama of spirit with implications reaching far into eternity, as the soul responds to this invitation to a wider gift of self to God through complete dedication to Christ. Such a direct challenge can be met only with a courageous, unswerving generosity, that spirit of consumed consecration discovered in those who yearn to love God with all their hearts, all their minds, and all their strength.

Surely more and more of our young men and women will step forward to answer this challenge as its terms are rendered more explicit to their understanding in a modern context. We speak often of the serious dearth of religious vocations in our present era; awesome statistics are quoted, underlining the very real problems frustrating the steady growth of the Church in America because of a seeming lack of souls willing to give themselves to Christ and His service in this way. Yet, as the author emphasizes so well, "vocational ignorance is at least partly responsible for this critical situation." Father Butler will, in the pages that follow, indicate forcefully the

reasons for this contemporary decline in religious vocations, as well as concisely outline the pattern of
Divine Providence in the shaping of a religious vocation in the individual soul. Fortunately, Father Butler's scholarship is never tedious; his simple style is
the result of ten years of the active apostolate among
young men and women in Catholic colleges and
state universities, as well as his advanced theological
research on vocations.

Of special interest is the stress placed by the
author on the strictly demanded qualifications in the
possible candidate for the religious novitiate, and
his brilliant exposition of the delicate topic of the
so-called "lost vocation." Without losing his readers
in a maze of psychological jargon, Father Butler
shows precisely how subjective dispositions towards
religious dedication may be tempered by personal
inadequacies of mental, physical, or moral condition-
ing: he demonstrates in indisputable terms that natural motives are not enough for a lasting religious
consecration, that superficial attractions are easily
dissipated in the crucible of religious self-sacrifice.
If directors of souls heed just this one prudent counsel, then this slim volume will have served its fundamental purpose most admirably.

We are sincerely grateful to Father Butler, com-
mending him on this accomplished work. It is our

prayer also that this splendid book will serve as an effective instrument of Divine Grace so that through its thoughtful reading, again in the words of the author . . . "the generous and courageous, resolving to enter religious life, will do so with tranquil and serene conviction—with the unruffled serenity of a fool for Christ."

MOST REVEREND EDWIN VINCENT BYRNE, D.D.
Archbishop of Santa Fe

RELIGIOUS VOCATION
AN UNNECESSARY MYSTERY

"For there are eunuchs who were born so from their mother's womb; and there are eunuchs who were made so by men; and there are eunuchs who have made themselves eunuchs for the kingdom of heaven. He that can take, let him take it."

—Matthew 19:12

CHAPTER I

The Unnecessary Mystery

RELIGION has always had elements of mystery in it. And so it should. The chasm between God and man is infinite, unlimited. There must always be areas unexplored, unexplained, in some instances, frankly inexplicable. In facing God, man's encounter with a veil of mystery is inevitable.

The simple soul may, and does, oversimplify his contact with his creator. The primitive man establishes that contact by the rhythm of his feet pounding the earth, the repetitious beat of his drum, the hypnotic monotony of his chant. The modern sentimentalist makes God in his own image, and constructs a homey, avuncular character, benign and blandly tolerant, who deserves an occasional recognition equivalent to the salute of a flag. The orthodox Christian finds a comforting contact in the little way of a St. Francis or a St. Therese, but usually he fails to reach the profundity necessarily associated with such simplicity.

Nevertheless the inescapable fact remains that

1

God, both in His transcendence over the world and His immanence in it, remains a mystery to the mind of man. The approach to God through nature demands a concept of analogy, a realization that even with valid deductions about the Author of Nature we are achieving a knowledge of dissimilarities more than similarities. St. Thomas Aquinas, who perhaps pursued the knowledge of God more intently than any other inquirer, stated bluntly that the investigation of God through natural reason leads more to a knowledge of what God is *not,* rather than to what He is.

Pagan cults at least faced this conclusion frankly and offered what has been aptly called "mystery religions." These promoted the accepted occult nature of man's relation to God and consequently proposed varying systems of symbols to provide for a lack of direct contact. Pagan man knew, more by reasonable conjecture than by blind instinct, that he was a responsible creature of the Unknown God.

Direct contact was established by God Himself through revelation, literally the drawing back of the veil of the Godhead. Even so, the veil was drawn only gradually and only in part. From the progenitors of the human race, through the patriarchs and the prophets, to the promised fulfillment in the God-Man, Jesus Christ, the secrets of God's life, and our own in relation to Him, were imparted only when necessary and in terms which could be understood. The vision of God, and all things in Him, the beatific goal of human life, require an altogether new mode of knowledge which is supernatural because it is immediate and eternal.

Until then we can see only "through a glass, darkly," exploring theologically the deposit of revelation. Even more, we are given the Holy Spirit to enlighten us, to infuse the human mind with divine wisdom. This is so much more fruitful than the theological gropings of faith that the Prince of Theologians, after the experience of such infused knowledge, had to say, by comparison, "All that I have written is straw."

And still the elements of mystery remain. We say that certain matters of faith are supernatural mysteries, accepted on the authority of God's revelation, but beyond the reach of natural reason to comprehend. The principal mysteries of Christian faith, as the catechism teaches, are the Incarnation and the Trinity. But, as a matter of fact, we recognize the mystery of all of God's dealings with us when, even in revelation, we recall the many scenes of the drama of our Redemption in the recitation of the Rosary as "mysteries."

St. Paul, almost in exasperation, expresses the

necessity of divine mystery, even after revelation, in his words to the Romans (II Epistle, 11: 33-36): "Oh, the depth of the riches of the wisdom and of the knowledge of God! How incomprehensible are his judgments and how unsearchable his ways! For who has known the mind of the Lord, or who has been his counsellor? Or who has first given to him, that recompense should be made him? For from him and through him and unto him are all things. To him be the glory forever, amen."

The mind of man, however, tends to multiply mysteries unnecessarily. Given the light, he often prefers darkness. Perhaps it is just a natural tendency to intellectual sloth: whatever is difficult to grasp I will dismiss as mystery; a mystery is inexplicable and therefore does not require, since it cannot achieve, thorough understanding. Or perhaps there is a deeper psychological motive. There may be a subconscious desire for mystery in man's search for God. If this is based on a humble acknowledgement of the divine omniscience, the motivation may be good. If, on the other hand, the basis is an irresponsible escape into the shadows of mystery, to the neglect of an obligated examination of revelation given for exploration, such an intellectual retreat is deplorable and culpable.

Notice how people have always flocked to the

sites of reported celestial apparitions, or how they manifest concern for occult information, such as the content of the letter written by Lucy of Fatima. Yet these same people are often those most guilty of neglecting the study of Christian doctrine as it is derived from public revelation in the deposit of faith, preserved and daily taught through multiple available means by the Church.

Religious vocation—the call to follow Christ by observing His counsels as well as His commands—is a matter of public revelation. The human response to this divine invitation is a matter of public history. And yet an aura of mystery has beclouded this simple invitation in the popular mind to the point of complication and confusion for both the observer of and the participant in religious life—an established state in which one can achieve, more safely and securely, the common Christian goal of perfection in charity.

The confusion, even consternation, experienced by those outside the Church is at least understandable. Undiluted Christian doctrine clearly teaches the ultimate advantages of virginity, the poverty of detachment and the obedient submission of the will to divine authority, directly or by delegation. But to the modern mind, which is generally indifferent to religion, these achievements are the antitheses of secular success. The tolerance of sexual immorality and exaggerated concern for romantic love, the drive for monetary and material gain, and the distorted individualism which characterize our times inspire an abhorrence for their opposites, which comprise the essential means of religious life.

I deliberately speak of *means* because observers, both in and out of the Church, often view poverty, chastity and obedience as the ends or goals of religious life. These practices are, as will be emphasized later, only means and not ends in themselves. They are the best possible means of attaining the common Christian vocation of perfection in charity. Undoubtedly many will admire, without emulating, the simplicity and detachment of St. Francis. But too many do so without seeing these qualities as conditions required for a higher goal, the ultimate goal of union with God through supernatural love. We are fools for Christ's sake, not for the sake of foolishness. To be voluntarily poor, chaste, and submissive without transcendent purpose would be the height of foolishness in this world. Too many people outside of the fold look at those in religious life from a purely natural point of view and understandably shy away. You can see the hostility in the eyes of the unbeliever, or the uninformed, glancing at the serene nuns seated in the subway.

But there are also too many within the Church

who shy away for other reasons. Rather than look askance, they exalt religious life to a super-mysterious level which is altogether unnecessary and definitely undesirable. As a matter of fact, their interpretation, or lack of it, of religious vocation is detrimental to the further increase or success of these vocations. They make religious life as unnatural as the secularist does, perhaps more so. They fail to understand the supernatural and distort, by divorcing, its relation to the natural. They are guilty of promoting the unnecessary mystery.

The specific crime is that of relegating religious vocation to the realm of Gnosticism, making of it an esoteric private inspiration. At least that is the unmistakable tone of their conversation and propaganda on the subject. The general offense, and it is a popular fault, is a lack of clarification in a matter which requires theological precision. And this is a grave matter, directly affecting the salvation of souls. Religious life is not an extra, not a luxury, not a peculiar path for exceptional souls in the pursuit of Christian perfection. It is necessary for the apostolic work of the Church and for the personal salvation of some of its members. The mystery, and consequent confusion, which has been added to the essential notion of religious vocation is unnecessary and dangerous.

That this mystery *has* been added is a patent fact

to the theologian who examines the plethora of propaganda about religious vocations. Without citing specific sources, and thereby embarrassing their authors, let me quote just a few obscure and misleading suggestions offered to the magnanimous youth who desires to follow the counselled path of the Master.

We have to sympathize with the perplexed young soul, pondering an eternal future and seeking a safer route, who is vaguely instructed: "My dear friend, in your heart of hearts, ask yourself if God is not calling you." The anxious reader of such advice is sent out on a scavenger hunt for a divine communication. His search is bound to be futile. He is not sure, and neither am I, exactly what one's "heart of hearts" is. He does not know where to look, or, for that matter, what to look for. What is this "call?" How do you get it? And how do you know when you have it?

All that can be gleaned from most of the popular propaganda and discussion on the subject is that a religious vocation is very special; an indescribable communication, which God suddenly slips into an unexpected, and consequently unhappy, soul. And that selected person, apparently, is arrested by this heavenly message, raised out of his or her customary condition and placed at the crossroads of decision with an insistent demand from the Commanding

Chief for a decisive answer to this divine summons.

Further, if we follow the propaganda line, we discover that the unsuspecting and uneasy soul is pounced upon at some particular point of time. The call somehow comes and the befuddled recipient now "has a vocation"—with all the misery unnecessarily consequent upon it. There are even implied threats for the one who hesitates or hangs back. Again a random quotation to illustrate my charge: "One who has such a vocation has a special gift from God. There are early, middle and late vocations. Each one should take God's gift whenever He offers it; otherwise it may be withdrawn." Such gifted souls are left to agonies of indecision which make them wish they were like the rest of men. And you can't blame them.

Few writers on religious vocation ever attempt to define, even by description, just what this vocation is. Vocational counsellors in secular professions do not share this difficulty. But when it comes to religious profession the curtain of confusion comes down and the actors speak empty phrases in hushed whispers. Many volumes have been written on the subject of religious vocation, but I have yet to find any presumed authority on the subject who can be pinned down to a precise statement or a clear definition. Most circumvent the problem of specific mean-

ing and are content with general clichés. There is a
definite intimation of a heart-stir because they use
such phrases as "feeling drawn," "is attracted," "feels
within herself a desire," "feels a strong attraction."
No wonder the ordinary aspirant seeks a vocation
inside himself, like a doctor probing for an inflamed
appendix.

The insistence upon an overwhelming feeling, or
upon some sentimental something, can reach poetic
extremes. Allow me a choice quotation of this type:
"The call to Religious Life [please note the impressive capital letters] comes in various ways. In some
cases it is distinct and overpowering. In others, it
is gentle, like a whispering breeze, and must be
listened to carefully in order to be discerned."

The image conjured in the average reader's mind
is that of a dour damsel by a wooded stream, standing silently with a cocked ear cupped by one hand
while the other hand is extended to buffer the blow
of the awaited wind of seizure. Let me say, in case
a writer recognizes his own lines, I have not singled
out the quotations I have used for particular criti-
cism. They have been chosen at random and merely
illustrate a common terminology and mode of expression in current literature on the subject.

There is, of course, an element of truth in all of
these citations. Nevertheless there is contained in

them a dangerous implication, a misdirection and bewilderment which can only do harm to the Church and her members. It is unfortunate, to say the least, that our popular concept of religious vocation is so vague and unexplained. But worse still is the tag of exclusiveness usually attached to this notion. There is, of course, an ultimate mystery here, the mystery of divince predilection and therefore a certain individual exclusiveness in God's dealing with all men; but that should not enter into a specific discussion of religious vocation. Might as well talk about the mystery of predestination and be done with it!

This supposition, repeated and emphasized, of something both obscure and special in religious vocation is certainly foreign to the mind and expressed doctrine of the principal theologian of the Church, St. Thomas Aquinas. A scholar on the subject of religious vocation, and confrere of the Angelic Doctor, pointed this out some time ago and warned of the dangers consequent upon such a distortion of sound theology.

The contemporary ways of considering religious vocation, although diverse and opposed among themselves, also have this point in common: that they suppose it to be something quite rare, even exceptional in the Christian life. This is a supposition as gratuitous as it is dangerous; for once admitted it is not possible to divorce it from its consequences, which just about amount to the total suppression of religious life. (Marianus Maggiolo, O.P., *"La Vocazione Religiosa, Secondo S. Tommaso," Xenia Thomistica*, Rome, 1925, II, 280.)

Unfortunately the gratuitous and dangerous supposition does not remain upon the printed page or on the lips of the indoctrinated counsellor. This supposition creates a disturbing impression on the sensitive souls of generous young men and women who are groping their way up the ladder of Christian perfection. Confusion gives way to hesitation and doubt, even discouragement and despair, in approaching religious life. If this vocation is for a select few who receive an indescribably divine invitation can the humble soul dare to assume that he has received such a special gift? This is a grave problem, personal and permanent. For religious vocation is indissolubly linked to the certain vocation of all to Christian perfection.

When the anxious aspirant approaches a priest for vocational guidance the problem becomes a mutual one. For the priest is God's minister, the interpreter of His word and the dispenser of His gifts. And this is not a light matter, easily dismissed, but one of profound concern, affecting both the doubtful soul and the director of souls in doubt. The inevitable question will be: "Father, how can I tell whether or not I have a religious vocation; how can I be sure?" The question must go unanswered if the idea of vocation is hazy and indefinite in the mind of the director. Too often the question is treated with impressive circumlocution and the injunction to pray over the problem, as though the sincere inquirer had not considered such a fundamental Christian course and as though confirming his false expectation of a direct divine communication. Later the puzzled petitioner realizes he is back where he started, as mixed up over his problem as he was before.

The counsellor, of course, cannot make up the inquirer's mind for him and risk a vicarious decision of such import. He seeks a ready solution which is not available. There is no certain formula or norm which can be employed. One cannot expect a standard of pigeon-hole precision in a subject so broad and encompassing. This is a matter of theology, and psychology, applied to the moral actions of a particular personality. We should not expect the Church to formulate every judgment in every Christian conscience. Some seem to express such foolhardy expectation; one writer even complains that there is an absence of "a discretionary norm of easy and sure application, with the exception of a few directives and laws fixed by the authority of the

Church with regard to certain limited cases." Does the complaining author want an IBM reply to the request of Miss Stella G.?

In moral matters the teaching office of the Church is exercised in the clarification of principles, not in the application of every principle to every particular practice. We are allowed, in fact required, to think and judge for ourselves. No wonder the teaching authority of the Church is so distorted in the mind of the non-Catholic. Much of this distortion is our own fault.

The obvious task required is a restatement of the theological principles involved. This book will say nothing new, only repeat what has been forgotten or is unknown. Only in the light of these revealed principles can the darkness of confusion be dispelled, the anguish of the aspirant to religious life be allayed. We must use enlightened prudence in alleviating what Father Juan Ortega, O.P., calls "the torment of simple souls, animated by good desires of being religious and with aptitude for being such, who do not succeed in satisfying themselves that such is the will of God." (*La Vocacion Religiosa,* Universidad de Sto. Tomas. Manila, 1947, p. 20.)

The key to the solution of this contemporary problem lies, as a matter of fact, in this expressed anxiety to do the will of God. It is precisely in the revealed doctrine of the nature of the divine will that we will obtain a clear concept of vocation to the religious state or, more precisely, to Christian perfection. And in this context we can destroy the gratuitous and dangerous notion that religious vocation is a rare gift and esoteric in its realization. We can also discover, in this part of theology, certain normative principles to apply personally to the aspirant to the religious state of life.

There will always be elements of mystery in religion; for "who has known the mind of the Lord; who has been His counsellor?" Yet God has deigned to speak to man, to withdraw a bit the veil of mystery by His revelation. That revelation is contained in the traditional teaching of the Church, drawn from the inspired Scriptures, the commentaries of the Fathers, the theology of the Doctors, the infallible decisions of the Magisterium of the Church. Only by neglecting sound theology, and turning instead to the rhetoric of sentiment, have we made an unnecessary mystery of religious vocation. And we have done so to the detriment of generous souls who aspire to dedicate themselves to the service of God through the religious state of life.

Before examining the theology of religious vocation it may help to look back historically to the development of religious life from the formation of the primitive Christian community to the present condition of that state and the current concept of vocation to it.

CHAPTER II

How It Happened

WHEN asked which was the greatest command-
ment, Our Lord immediately enunciated the precept of charity, to love God above all and one's
neighbor as one's self. Perfection in charity is, without question, the primary precept and common goal
of the followers of Christ.

Jesus clearly distinguished between command
and counsel, between end and means. The safer and
more direct way of observing the primary precept
and attaining the desired end of Christian life is by
means of the counsels: voluntary virginity, poverty
of spirit and obedience to the will of God and the
Christian community. His counsel to the rich young
man was in response to the question of the average
Christian, "What is yet wanting to me?" To be a
eunuch for the sake of the kingdom of God is not
for all, but "let him accept it who can."

Yet from the beginning of the Church the early
Christians strove to fulfill counsel as well as com-

mand, or, better still, to observe the counsels in order to obey the commandments. The primitive Christian community was the prototype of the contemporary religious community. Especially was this true with regard to communal life and the required sacrifice of individual possessions. In the primary source of early Church history (Acts of the Apostles: 5: 32-35) we read about the manner of life of these early Christians: "Now the multitude of the believers were of one heart and one soul, and not one of them said that anything he possessed was his own, but they had all things in common. And with great power the apostles gave testimony to the resurrection of Jesus Christ our Lord. Nor was there anyone among them in want. For those who owned land or houses would sell them and bring the price of what they sold and lay it at the feet of the apostles, and distribution was made to each, according as anyone had need."

This arrangement was feasible with a small group of Christian believers living together in community. Later, however, with the spread of Christianity throughout the known world, such universal communal life was impractical. But what is noteworthy is that the primitive Christian observed the evangelical counsels as a matter of course, with a responsibility gravely binding and accepted. Consider the sudden awful fate of Ananias and Sapphira when they reneged and held back! Surely no one of these first followers of Christ hesitated over the stumbling block of religious vocation, wondering whether they were called to observe the counsels or not.

Out of these primitive Christian communities came the heroic martyrs who dared to defy the pre-eminence of paganism and wrote their testimony of faith in blood, the physical sacrifice of their lives as witnesses to the revelation of Christ. Only after Constantine and the Edict of Milan in the fourth century did such martyrdoms cease, save for the few months of the reign of Julian the Apostate.

Then a new Christian era began, a period which brought new problems to the faithful: heresy, church-state conflict, the remnants of pagan immorality, the inevitable smouldering of the zeal fired by the immediate Apostles and disciples of Christ. As an antidote to this spiritual sickness a new movement came into the Church. It began in the East where these problems were very pronounced. The great exodus of Christians into the desert renewed and refreshed the ideal of Christian perfection.

Consider just how revolutionary this movement was! Frank Sheed, in his introduction to his edition of Helen Waddell's "The Desert Fathers" (pp. 18-19) describes the situation very well:

There were no monks or nuns as we know them now. The priesthood was not yet a distinct profession. The priest might be a married man with a family, he dressed like everyone else, and it was normal for him to earn his living by the practice of any trade or profession he had skill in. What we now take for granted as the religious life had made only small beginnings. Numbers — very considerable numbers it seems — of men and women had undertaken the celibate life and their prestige in the Christian body was second only to the martyrs whose example had been the great preservative of the Christian morale. These *continentes* did not at first live in communities but in their own homes. They fasted more than other Christians (all Christians then fasted more than we do), they spent long hours in prayer. They lived quietly, dressed quietly, gave themselves little or not at all to amusement. The works of charity were more and more entrusted to the *continentes*. From time to time groups of women vowed to continence would set up house together in a first beginning of the conventual life.

St. Antony was the key figure of this movement into the desert, the first known and prominent hermit who sought the cultivation of Christian perfection in solitude. He is also the best known to us because he had a biographer. St. Athanasius has provided us with a detailed account of the man and his life. Others rushed to follow his example of asceticism. By 325, the time of the Council of Nicea, there were over 5000 solitaries, women as well as men, in the Desert of Nitria. They were hermits, living alone and coming together only for the celebration of Mass.

Another kind of religious life, more the kind that we know today, arose at about the same time. St. Pachomius founded the first monasteries, communities of men living together under a common rule of life to achieve their mutual goal, perfection in Christian charity. They were called cenobites. The first of these monasteries was located in Tabenna in Egypt. For centuries thereafter the monastic life meant either being a hermit or a cenobite.

St. Basil, who travelled up the Nile in the middle of the fourth century, recognized and reported the weaknesses of the monastic life which he observed. The cenobitic system of Pachomius, he said, was too complex and impersonal. Tabenna was a town, practically an armed camp, a boisterous and undisciplined community of five thousand ascetics.

The inhabitants were even divided up into platoons and regiments under a hierarchy of military officials led by the abbot who was a kind of commander-in-chief. Much of the ascetic practice was either brutally imposed or vainly exhibited. There was no intimate contact with superiors, no spiritual direction, no reasonable rule to follow. Only the orthodox spirituality of some of the monks salvaged a degree of success from this mass movement to embrace a form of religious life.

Again, from the historical fragments extant, we have no indication of a vocational problem. If anything, there was insufficient reflection on the purpose of their pursuit by many who fled to the desert.

St. Benedict, in the sixth century, formulated a sound rule of religious life which still serves as a conventual rule for many communities today. He shifted the emphasis from physical to spiritual mortification and focused on the end of religious life as distinct from the means of fulfilling it. His motto, *Pray and Work,* signified a sound and simple approach to the pursuit of Christian perfection. Benedict's monks, with their quiet simplicity and faithful guardianship of the classical tradition of assiduous study, mental prayer and the dignity of manual labor, were a steadying influence on the Church, so violently rocked by the barbarian invasion.

Religious life then developed with some stability. From time to time reforms were needed, in the monasteries as well as within the general membership of the Church. The Dark Ages, the period of the barbarian invasions, was a time of spiritual desolation and only the monastic communities succeeded in preserving Christian culture, but even they were affected by the general decline of spiritual and moral values. Religious life prospered or declined accordingly, in direct proportion to the vicissitudes of the Church.

A very significant development occurred in the thirteenth century with the coming of the friars: the establishment of the mendicant orders, particularly the Franciscans and the Dominicans. Religious life assumed new forms and functions. Instead of being confined to the work of worship in single monasteries, the friars moved from one community house to another and engaged in apostolic work outside of their convents. They assumed intellectual leadership in the great universities of Europe. They taught and wrote and preached, the latter function a former prerogative of bishops. They organized democratic government in their houses and left the cloister to spread the faith in mission fields. At the same time, convents of women were founded, and both contemplative nuns and sisters engaged in active work: catechetics, nursing, visiting the poor and giving maternal care to orphans. Religious life began to assume the complexity and variety of structure and function which we know today.

Every order, congregation or society of religious has its particular purpose; each is a different facet in the jewel of dedicated Christian life. Often they were founded to offset and oppose some social evil which was hostile and detrimental to the life of the Church; the Benedictines opposed military might with the power of interior peace; Franciscans fought worldly indulgence with the power of poverty of spirit; Dominicans attacked heresy with the power of knowledge, both sacred and profane; Jesuits led the counter-offensive after the Reformation with the power of spiritual discipline and enlightened faith. Yet these were not altogether negative forces, for each religious foundation offered its own particular mode of positive spirituality with appropriate means.

Religious life flourished in the Middle Ages. Nearly every city and town had its monastery or convent, physically and spiritually dominating the locality with a prominence befitting the living example of the fullness of faith, the practice of both the counsels and commands of Christ. Youths from every station of life knocked on the doors of religious houses seeking admission. They did not ask whether or not they "had a vocation."

The number of those adopting the religious state as a way of life has not diminished since the Middle Ages. There are an estimated 300 thousand men and

800 thousand women in religious life today.* Perhaps the proportionate figure is lower, but life is not as simple now as it was in medieval society, and vocations of all kinds have multiplied and variegated to satisfy the needs of the complex structure of modern life. Though the rate of religious vocations rises and falls there is no observable decline, only a marked recognition of a greater need for religious men and women to care for the various and increasing apostolic functions of the Church today.

As Andre Frossard says (in his *The Salt of the Earth* p. 13): "The rhythm of the various foundations remains steady, unaffected by revolutions and wars. But, just as an epidemic gives rise to a quickening of self-sacrifice, so some law of justice seems to balance a collapse of ethics and ideals by an increase in vocations, and while conquerors, politicians and prophets of a new social order believe themselves capable of changing the balance of power and of inflecting the course of history, an invisible factor gently re-establishes the equipoise without their knowledge."

Considering the vocational controversy which has engendered so much confusion during the past century, it is remarkable that the influx of postulants to religious life has remained constant.* There is no historical indication of such controversy prior to the

---

* These statistics are from 1961, just before the drastic decline in the number of priests and religious which took place after Vatican Council II (1962-1965). —*Publisher*, 2005.

nineteenth century. While the important decision to renounce the world for the cloister has always been a personal problem of magnitude, demanding as it does a complete reversal of secular values and the adoption of an altogether new way of life for the postulant, there is no evidence on record that an objective problem concerning the nature of religious vocation existed until recent times.

The older theologians never treated this problem precisely as it is proposed today. The insinuation of the moderns that one should subject himself to deep self-analysis (even the canned psychoanalysis of prepared tests today), and prolonged deliberation over whether or not one has "the call," represents a definite departure from the sound teaching of St. Thomas Aquinas that no one should delay, or even deliberate over, a simple resolve to enter religious life. In fact, he says, don't seek advice except from those who will encourage you!

The only impediment to entering religious life considered by St. Jerome was the physical obstacle of a father lying prostrate across the threshold to prevent a child from entering the cloister; and in this case, St. Jerome advised stepping over him to fulfill this holy resolve and get to the convent. St. Thomas considered only a few prohibitive impediments, such as grave illness, heavy debts—or having a wife!

On the other hand, contemporary theologians not only make a problem of the objective nature of religious vocation, but, among themselves, are in much disagreement as to the treatment and solution of this manufactured problem. As a recent research scholar on the problem has said: "To consult the tracts on religious vocation in the classical manuals of moral theology is to court confusion; for authors are not all agreed, not even on essentials." (Fr. Edward P. Farrell, O.P., *The Theology of Religious Vocation*, p. 5.)

How did this happen?

The crux of the contemporary problem has its foundation in the perennial controversy over the nature of the movement of actual grace. It's a reflection, of course, over the old theological conflict over the respective roles of the divine will and the human will in the operation of grace. One must keep in mind that whatever an author holds on this basic question of divine grace and human choice will decide his particular doctrine on the nature of religious vocation. The simple fact is that God acts divinely and we act humanly, and precisely how these two actions coincide in all that we do is a necessary mystery. It would be nice if people let it go at that. People do, but professional theologians do not.

The critical point in the development of this controversy occurred in France during the last century. The French seem to have a knack for getting involved in disputes, theological or otherwise. Anyway, certain French theologians and spiritual writers popularized an attraction theory in resolving religious vocations. They taught that in a divine vocation, both to the priesthood and to the religious life, the essential and decisive element is a mystical attraction. *"L'attrait,"* they called it, and described it as an instinctive and even sensible propulsion, an internal compulsion that makes itself known, a mystical phenomenon—even "a sweet impulse," a "secret voice." (Now you know where those fuzzy quotations cited in the first chapter came from.)

Then, dear Reader, the theological sparks began to fly. Two books appeared, one in 1909 and the other in 1910, by Canon Lahitton refuting the proponents of the attraction theory. The attractionists, if we may call them that, were quite perturbed, to say the least. They struck back and demanded that the canon's vocational works be submitted to Rome for examination, and, they hoped, for condemnation. The champions of the inner-voice theory suffered defeat when the Commission reported negatively; that is, they freed Canon Lahitton's works from the stigma of condemnation. The following year (1913) directive norms on the subject of religious vocation were issued with the approval of Pope Pius X. These norms clearly denied the necessity of a feeling of attraction as the decisive factor in the recognition of a religious vocation.*

One might think that that would have settled the matter, but theological controversies die hard and always leave the stamp of the conflicting opinions on the popular mind.

While the Holy See decided in favor of Canon Lahitton's publications, in the sense that they were not subject to condemnation, the Commission did not intend a blanket approval of everything contained in these books. And, as a matter of fact, Canon Lahitton, in his zeal to eradicate the attraction theory, leaned too far in the opposite direction. The oversimplifying Canon, carrying others in his wake, settled for what is best called "juridical, or ecclesiastical, vocation"—the call to ordination by an ordaining bishop or acceptance of a postulant by a legitimate superior—as the complete interpretation of sacerdotal or religious vocation. Disregarded were the necessary particular and antecedent graces involved in any series of supernatural actions. In other

---

* See p. 104 of this book. —*Publisher*, 2005.

words, the very necessary mystery of God's action through grace was ignored, in fact, positively excluded; and that's making matters altogether too unmysterious.

As a result of this doctrinal clash over the question of vocation, different schools of thought began to develop and to promote their particular theories. The extremes represented overemphasized either the divine action or the human action in the development of a vocation to God's service. Numerous distinctions were proposed, such as "external" and "internal" vocation, "general" and "special" grace. Scriptural texts were conveniently adapted to fit the proposed opinion and St. Thomas Aquinas, always a good authority to cite, was claimed as the forerunner of opposite camps. Even St. Thomas Aquinas and St. Alphonsus Liguori were pitted against each other, when actually, understanding of their terminology correctly, shows that they agreed on the subject.

All of these opinions, unfortunately, have been frequently repeated in popular writings on the subject of vocation. There is even the failure to distinguish carefully between sacerdotal vocation and religious vocation—that is, between a priest's vocation and vocation to the religious state of life. I intend, by the way, to confine my concern to religious vocation only, with merely by-the-way reference to sacerdotal vocation.

So that is how it happened. A theological dispute occurred which has since seeped into popular propaganda, to the consequent confusion of the sincere inquirer and the responsible counsellor.

We now have a maze of conflicting theories, all of which are deficient and misleading. Lined up they can be categorized as follows: (1) Vocation properly consists in a mystical attraction, an inner compulsion, felt in the depths of the soul. (2) Vocation properly consists in the call of an ordaining bishop or, in the case of religious, admittance by a legitimate superior. (3) For some there is a special vocation through special gifts of grace; for others the general call of the counsels, without particular grace, suffices for entrance; the grace of perseverance comes by the petition of prayer. (4) All that is necessary for a religious vocation is general grace, harnessed, as it were, by the human will to the pursuit of this goal; the resolve of the will is antecedent to any divine decree and particular grace.

These are the erroneous opinions—which we will avoid. Let us return to the sound doctrine of the fathers and doctors of the Church. We have dealt with confusion long enough. We only wanted to show you how it happened, how a clear idea became confused in the popular mind. The time has come for clarity, for a re-examination of traditional sound doctrine on the nature of religious vocation.

Let's make a fresh—which in reality is an old—approach to the understanding of the concept of religious vocation. In this way we can dispel the unnecessary mystery which we have inherited from modern controversialists.

CHAPTER III

Approach to Understanding

GRANTED that a problem has been created, a mystery concocted, over the nature of religious vocation; how should we approach it in order to acquire understanding? Surely the proper approach is not through the maze of current popular opinion on the subject. That would only be courting confusion further. And yet the problem cannot be ignored or neglected because of its pertinence to Christian life as a whole and its personal significance to every generous youth who ponders the magnanimous question; "What is yet wanting to me?"

The desirable route of research, in this instance, is backwards, through sound theology to the sources of revelation, to a rediscovery and restatement of the teaching of the Church, speaking for Christ, on the role of religious life in the Redemption of the faithful. A correct theology of religious vocation must be recovered and reiterated. But this can be done only by placing the elements of the problem into the whole context of theology. For this problem, precisely as it is stated today, is an artificial one, compounded of elements which should be studied singly and in proper reference to the whole divine plan of Redemption.

This is a gigantic task, to be sure, and yet one which has to be undertaken in at least a summary form with an emphasis on essentials. Only in this way can we hope to reach a satisfactory understanding and solution to the problem. There is no simple formula for religious vocation in the official teaching of the Church. As a matter of fact, the two key words, "religious" and "vocation," have different points of reference and never appear together in Sacred Scripture, in the commentaries of the Fathers, in the theology of the Doctors, or in the law of the Church. The phrase appears only in modern manuals and involves a juxtaposition of different ideas and the appropriation of terms that are analagous.

Indeed, the term *religious* refers to a state of life. A state of life, according to St. Thomas, implies a fixed establishment in the spiritual life, with reference to some solemn obligation, and is properly applied to the state of perfection. Those, he says, who have a special obligation to tend to spiritual perfection are thereby in a state of perfection. In this state, however, he includes only religious, those under perpetual vows, and bishops, by the nature of their office.

St. Augustine proposes a broader sense of the phrase, extending it to those constituted in the spiritual life by ecclesiastical power or by a sacrament. He lists in this category the married, clerics, religious and prelates. St. Antoninus admits an improper sense of "state of life" which can apply to permanent duties and professions.

Religious, organized as they are to undertake solemn religious obligations, come under the special jurisdiction of the Church. From the laws of the Church regulating religious life one is able to compose the following canonical definition of it:

"A state wherein one makes profession of tending to perfection—a form of life, approved by the Church, wherein some of the faithful, joined in a society, establish themselves in order to tend to perfection by means of the three vows of poverty, chastity and obedience, which they make according to a Rule." (Thus Peter Cotel, S. J., "The Catechism of the Vows," p. 26.)

The essential idea, therefore, is that religious are those in the religious state, and assume a special obligation to tend towards Christian perfection by means of the vows of religion. These vows are founded upon an absolute acceptance of the three general counsels given by Christ: "And there are eunuchs who have made themselves so for the sake of the kingdom of heaven. Let him accept it who can." (Matt. 19:12); "If thou wilt be perfect, go, sell what thou hast, and give to the poor, and thou shalt have treasure in heaven; and come, follow me." (Matt. 19:21). The counsel founding the vow of obedience, says St. Thomas, is contained in the challenge "Come, follow me."

Nonetheless, the faithful following of Christ is an obligation incumbent upon all Christians, so that none can ignore these counsels. Thus St. Thomas distinguishes an exterior perfection, made manifest by the absolute undertaking of the counsels, to which all are not held, from that of an interior perfection of love of God and neighbor to which all *are* bound. While the letter of the counsels does not always obligate all men, the spirit of abnegation of all impediments to one's love of God *does* always oblige all men.

An important point is immediately evident. All Christians are obliged to tend toward Christian perfection,* and in some way through the observance of the evangelical counsels. The spirit of detachment is essential to spiritual progress. Some voluntarily

---

* For more on the universal obligation to advance toward Christian perfection, see Fr. Garrigou-Lagrange, O.P., *The Three Ages of the Interior Life*, Vol. 1 (1947; TAN, 1989), pp. 202 ff. —*Publisher*, 2005.

place themselves in a state where this obligation becomes fixed and regulated and the counsels are observed absolutely and literally. These latter are those we call religious.

The word "vocation," as it is used in the phrase "religious vocation," presents much more difficulty; in fact, it is of the essence of the problem.

In popular usage, "vocation" sometimes refers to a state of life, actually the termination of a vocation in the strict sense. And so we speak of a person's "fidelity to his vocation." Or, in a still wider sense, we use the word with reference to jobs and professions. Hence we have vocational guidance programs and vocational schools. These are analogical uses, however, because vocation properly refers to that which antecedes and is terminated by a condition or state of life.

Etymologically, the word vocation is derived immediately from the Latin *vocare,* to call or to summon. In a less imperious sense it may mean to invite or to name. Hence a vocation is a bid or a summons, an invitation or a naming; and it is always expressed in some way because it is "voiced" (*vox*). An ordination to this term is implied in historical usage, giving the word the connotation of "Come here." This ordination is expressed and may be either mandatory or invitatory, manifesting the will of the speaker to another. More specifically, and properly, therefore, the word vocation means a manifestation or expression of another's ordination. And we do think of it in this proper sense when we now speak of religious vocation.

In Sacred Scripture God reveals His will to others by calling them. Sometimes this is a personal call directing some particular mission, such as the call to Samuel, or to the priesthood as Aaron was called. A whole group may be called to fulfill a special role in the drama of salvation, as Israel was called.

The use of call or vocation in the New Testament is restricted to the call to justification. Vocation is never used with reference to the counsels. This is a more recent appropriation by theologians, particularly of one text: "And those whom he has predestined, them he has also called, and those whom he has called, them he has also justified, and those whom he has justified, them he has also glorified." (Rom. 8:30.)

The Fathers of the Church commented extensively on the counsels. Whole tracts were written on virginity as a superior way of life. Most of these were specific commentaries on pertinent passages in Scripture. No consideration of vocation was attached to the practice of the counsels. Vocation was treated only in its proper reference to justification. The religious state in its fixed and organized form was not yet established and, as pointed out earlier, the counsels were practiced literally and absolutely by individual Christians within their own social community. The Fathers were concerned with the common Christian vocation to holiness of life through perfection in charity, and recognized the counsels for what they were—advised means to fulfill this common vocation more effectively, safely and directly. The problem of who should take these means was never considered by them. The divine dictum, "Let him accept it who can," was sufficiently clear to these early Church writers.

With the aid of these commentaries, the Doctors of the Church, in their more systematic theology, reasonably explicated what was implicit in the content of Scripture and Church teaching. These commentaries came at a later period in the history of the Church, a time when religious life as we know it had begun or was fully developed. When considering entrance into this state of life they spoke more firmly and positively than our contemporary scholars do. They discouraged prolonged deliberation by a postulant and even warned that for some, religious life was obligatory as the only safe means of attaining their salvation. The vocational problem, as posed today, was apparently unknown to them. St. Augustine even speculated contentedly over the prospect of all Christians following the evangelical counsels!

St. Thomas Aquinas, by official sanction pre-eminent among the Church's theologians, never treated, in any particular tract, the question of religious vocation as it is asked today. He did, however, have much to say about the counsels and the religious state. He devoted a number of questions in his *Summa Theologica* to the nature of religious perfection, discussing in particular both the religious state and entrance into it.[1]

The mind of St. Thomas, apparently, was free of the misty contemporary problem of searching for an intangible interior vocation—the "what-is-it" problem that has so vexed modern theologians and spiritual authors. In a single article,[2] he dismissed as quite unnecessary our contemporary emphasis on prolonged and dubious deliberation and frantic discussion about entering religious life. Also, in the *Summa*, he considered the counsels in themselves in a single brief article.[3] Vows, the termination of religious vocation, are treated under exterior acts of the virtue of religion.[4] Other considerations of the counsels can be found in the *Summa Contra Gentiles* and in his Scriptural commentaries, particularly those on the pertinent Gospel passages.[5] In his *Quodlibetales* he even discussed the particular question of children entering religious life—There's one for our conservative contemporaries to consider!

St. Thomas wrote three particular brief works in defense of and in praise of the religious state. These are (if you will excuse the Latin): *Contra Impugnantes Dei Cultum et Religionem, De Perfectione Vitae Spiritualis* and *Contra Pestifieram Doctrinam Retrahentium Homines a Religionis Ingressu.* That last title translated is a "shocker" for our contemporaries: "Against the Despicable Teaching of Those Preventing Men from Entering Religion."

These tracts in defense of religious life were written by St. Thomas during the long and bitter conflict between the seculars and regulars at the University of Paris. *Contra Retrahentes,* the culmination of his exposition of this topic and perhaps the closest particular approach to our present problem, was directed against those who would make a mystery and cause of doubt out of entrance into the religious state! This was the telling blow against the futile attempts of Gerard of Abbeville and Nicholas of Liseux, successors of William of St. Amor, to disparage the life and work of Dominicans and Franciscans at the University of Paris, the celebrated center of learning in Europe at that time. The motives of the antagonistic seculars in this dispute were tainted with jealousy over the success of the mendicant teachers in winning students, both in the classroom and into their orders.

As I said before, the particular modern problem of the nature of religious vocation plunges deeply into the whole synthesis of theology. For that reason, it cannot be solved satisfactorily except when seen in the context of the whole of theology. For example, much emphasis today is placed on what is called "internal vocation." This refers to the individual and personal response to the general invitation to the practice of the counsels given by Our Lord. For St. Thomas this simply meant a responsive act of the will (*propositum,* as he called it) or voluntary resolve, motivated by grace in the supernatural order and by divine providence in the natural order. This is a matter of divine movement in man's supernatural action. And St. Thomas presupposes familiarity with his sound doctrine on efficacious grace, so that his references to this divine efficacy are but brief phrases—as if to say "of course we take this for granted." St. Thomas never used the popular distinction of "general" and "special" grace; in fact, the implication of this distinction is highly suspect.

In approaching this problem I would prefer to avoid unnecessary distinctions. Much of the contemporary confusion on this subject is the result of multiplying terms and divisions to no avail. I would even like to avoid footnotes so as not to frighten the intellectually shy reader; but for the scholar who likes to check references I have already begun to number quotations from the works of St. Thomas and will list them in the back of the book. This will provide a handy compilation of Thomistic references on this subject for those who desire it.

I will not offer an apology but an *apologia,* a defense, of my almost exclusive use of the theology of St. Thomas Aquinas in solving this problem, or, if you will, unravelling this mystery. The Vicar of Christ has told us to "go to Thomas." Not one but many popes have directed us to follow the sound principles of St. Thomas in the solution of theological problems. In the current question of religious vocation we have a knotty theological problem which demands clarity and certitude. These qualities are assured by fidelity to the teaching of St. Thomas.

By anticipation let me say that there are two essential notes in a religious vocation: a divine invitation and a human acceptance or response. Because of man's necessary dependence in every motion, however, God not only invites but also moves the subject to respond. He does so without violence to the freedom of human action, in both the natural and the supernatural orders. And so it is that we will consider religious vocation both on the part of God, in His counsel and operation, and on the part of man, under the supernatural and natural influences by which both God and man effect the truly human resolve to accept the divine counsel.

CHAPTER IV

The Divine Invitation

THE most agonizing question of the aspirant to religious life is "Do I have a vocation?" What he means, and he knows that he does, is "Is it God's will that I enter the religious state?" Or, more simply, "Is this what God wants me to do?" The question is agonizing because it's awfully important and, in a sense, unanswerable.

At least the inquirer is on the right track. If religious vocation is a divine ordination of a person to the religious state, then to know whether or not one is so ordained is to know God's will.

This is a common problem, one that we all experience. In everything that the conscientious Christian does, he desires to fulfill the divine will. He prays daily for this, as Our Lord instructed: "Thy will be done on earth as it is in heaven." He is mindful that this, or any prayer, cannot be divorced from the actual choices which he makes, because he remembers the warning of Christ: "Not everyone who says to me Lord, Lord, will enter the kingdom of heaven, but he who does the will of my father in heaven will enter the kingdom of heaven." The precise problem in particular actions is to know whether our will coincides with the divine will or not. To enter any permanent state of life, involving solemn obligations, is a choice one wants to make with divine approbation—even, and more accurately, by divine pre-ordination.

Interestingly, however, this concern for "having a vocation," in the sense of divine ordination to a state of life, is focused only on the religious state. Objectively, the married state presents many more difficulties and, as St. Paul says, divides a man's concern between creature and Creator. There are more dangers and less safeguards in seeking Christian perfection through this state of life. Yet I have never known of any young person fretting over whether or not he had a vocation to marriage. Nor have I ever noticed much doubt and deliberation, based on spiritual aspirations, expressed by those who contemplate marriage. The obvious implication is that we have shrouded the religious state with a veil of mystery that frightens a potential candidate. On the other hand, we apparently have neglected to show the married state in its true light of sacrifice and solemn obligation. The average youth, therefore, tends, in his own mind, to overemphasize or exaggerate the hardships of religious life and to minimize the burdens of marriage. This is somewhat aside, and yet to the point in our concern over God's will in making our own decisions.

The theological difficulty here is that God's will cannot be known directly, in itself. For God is utterly simple; that is, divisible only analagously and necessarily by the finite human mind probing divinity. God and His will are identified. So to know God's will directly is to know God directly. This kind of knowledge is possible only in the beatific vision, and when that is attained the problematic choices of this life are over.

Yet there are many who seem ignorant of this irrevocable fact. In their agonizing scrutiny, and this is especially true of some aspirants to religious life, they insist on "knowing for sure." The implication is that they must see the divine decree in their regard. This shows at least ignorance, at most presumption. We can know the eternal will of God only through its effects in time. On this important point all sincere Christians should be well-informed. Such knowledge is necessarily technical and profound, but worth every effort made to acquire it.

Theologians distinguish the divine will itself between the will of good pleasure (*voluntas bene-placiti*), which is identified with God and which we cannot see, and the divine will of sign or expression (*voluntas signi*), which represents the recognizable effects of God's will in time. As St. Thomas reminds us, the divine will of expression is a metaphorical assignation on our part, applied by way of likeness to what is properly an expression or sign of will in us.[7] The Angelic Doctor, in various places, makes a comprehensive division of these signs of divine will in relation to the divine will of good pleasure.[8] We will combine two of the three foundations he uses and see these external signs which reveal God's will. This is important, because in the five-part division of the divine will of expression we will see all the possible ways by which God's will is made known to us. The division shown on next page just about exhausts our knowledge of the divine will.

Well, there it is, a frankly formidable outline, but one which should be mastered by those who hope to understand how it is possible to know God's will in some measure. This is the only key to solving the vocational problem as currently posed.

These expressions of divine will, then, open the door to understanding the proper meaning of religious vocation. While it is true to say that vocation of any kind is a divine ordination, ultimately hidden in God's will of good pleasure, this ordination *is* "voiced" or expressed. We *can* know something

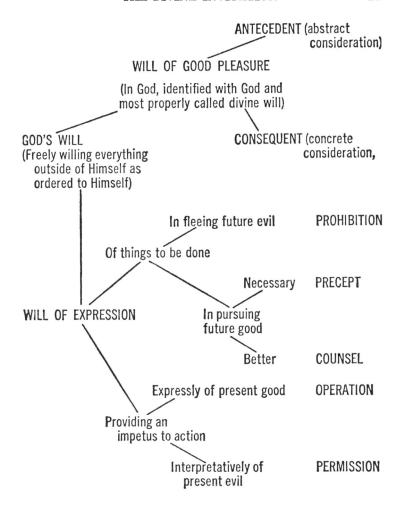

ANTECEDENT (abstract
consideration)

WILL OF GOOD PLEASURE
(In God, identified with God and
most properly called divine will)

GOD'S WILL
(Freely willing everything
outside of Himself as
ordered to Himself)

CONSEQUENT (concrete
consideration,

In fleeing future evil   PROHIBITION

Of things to be done

Necessary   PRECEPT

WILL OF EXPRESSION   In pursuing
future good

Better   COUNSEL

Expressly of present good   OPERATION

Providing an
impetus to action

Interpretatively of   PERMISSION
present evil

about it. Otherwise there could be no discussion of
divine vocation at all with any view to some practical procedure. And we can find that voicing, that
expression, through the divine governance which
executes such ordinations, that is, only in the tem-

poral effects of God's will—the will of sign or expression. And understanding of this divine will of expression provides the basic key to any problem pertaining to divine vocation—for that matter, to every action of God with respect to His creatures. Such understanding, I repeat, is worth every effort we make to acquire it.

Let's look at the outline again and see what it means.

The divine will of good pleasure is most properly the divine will, and this we do not see directly or in itself. The subdivision we make into antecedent and consequent simply indicates the difference between abstract and concrete considerations. Antecedently and abstractly God wills all men to be saved, just as a human judge wants all men to live. But consequently and concretely, considering the free human choices which are made, God saves only some of His people, just as the judge on the bench, in critical cases, allows only some of the criminals brought before him to live. In other words, we can look at the divine will prior to and consequent to what we do. God loves us and wants us to choose Him; but He permits us to abandon Him and suffer eternal estrangement. The divine will moves, but does not force, the human will in the direction we choose to take.

More important to us practically, and more familiar to us, is the expression of the divine will which we can recognize. God does manifest His will, instructing us as to what we should do. Before we act He reveals His will with regard to the evils we will face in the future and He prohibits them. Thus God clearly commands us to avoid the common obstacles to fulfilling the primary precept of love of God and neighbor. Hence there are prohibitions of evil, which impedes our vocation to perfection in charity, and precepts which command us to do what is good, primarily to love God and our neighbor wholeheartedly. The precepts tell us what we must do; these are not a matter of choice or preference. They are minimum requirements.

The rich young man put the question bluntly, "What . . . shall I do to have eternal life?" Christ replied with the minimum requirement— "If thou wilt enter into life, keep the commandments." The youth presses further: "All these I have kept; what is yet wanting to me?" Then Our Lord adds something more, a certain detachment and emptying of self which characterize His counsels. As we have said before, such a pure religious spirit is required in some degree of all Christians; to those who will accept it He asks for a literal and absolute practice of these counsels. In other words, such action is not

necessary but advisable as a better and safer procedure, a pursuit of definite goods and not just a retreat from evil.

God does not merely instruct us by revelation,
through His Church; He also and necessarily moves
us to do whatever we do. The divine will must provide the impetus to our actions or we could not act
at all. Every potency moved to act must be moved
by God, or else there would be no action. But He
moves us to moral action in different ways: positively and expressly He operates in us to do what is
good, both on natural and supernatural levels; interpretatively He permits us to do what is evil. It
is our choice, our responsibility, but without the dy-
namics of His action in us we could not change from
our ability to perform a bad action to our actually
doing it.

Now with regard to religious vocation we are obviously concerned with two particular effects of
God's will, His counsels and His operation in us
which enables us to respond to His invitation to
practice these counsels. According to St. Thomas,
two extrinsic principles promote the return of the
rational creature to God. These are law and grace.
Law, in a strict sense, is concerned with precept and
prohibition; in a wider sense it includes counsel as
a manifest ordination to an end. Divine operation

makes human action possible by its universal causality, through what we call premotion in the natural order and grace in the supernatural order. Hence in these effects of God's will we can trace the outline of religious vocation in the context of theology. To sharply delineate the precise theological position of religious vocation we must scrutinize closely these distinct elements, and first of all the ordination of counsel. This is what is sometimes called "exterior vocation."

In his *Summa Theologica*, St. Thomas treats the topic of divine counsel at the end of his tract on law. For counsel is a certain divine ordination manifested in the New Law and it partakes of the very nature of law. Yet counsel is not properly an act of law because it does not require any corresponding obligation.[9] Elsewhere he discusses the proper place of the counsels in the Christian life relative to the end of man—eternal beatitude.[10] For man stands between the things of this world and spiritual goods. And insofar as he adheres to the one he recedes from the other.

Man is drawn away from spiritual goods by three opposing concerns: things exterior to himself, such as wealth and material acquisitions ("the concupiscence of the eyes"), and to avoid these distractions Christ counsels poverty (Matt. 19:21)—things of the

body, such as carnal pleasure and solicitude for family ("the concupiscence of the flesh"), and to avoid
these divisive concerns Christ counsels virginity
(Matt. 19:12), as does St. Paul (I Cor., 7:25) and—
things of the soul, such as vanity and ambition ("the
pride of life"), and to avoid these selfish interests
Christ counsels obedience (Matt. 19:21), as does
St. Paul (Hebr. 8:17.) Because these three counsels
are dispositions for, and in practice, signs of, perfection, those who bind themselves to these counsels by vow are said to be in a state of perfection
and in a state of life which is fixed by solemn and
public obligation.

Now, it is of the utmost importance to perceive
the relation of the counsels to the precepts, and of
both to their mutual end—Christian perfection. St.
Thomas frequently, and at considerable length, reminds us of the proper place of the counsels in relation to the precepts and to perfection.[11] It would be
well for us to summarize this relation here, for it
has a strong bearing upon our subsequent notion of
religious vocation in the context of theology.

Christian perfection in itself is not a counsel but
a precept. "You therefore are to be perfect, even as
your heavenly Father is perfect." (Matt. 5:48.) This
perfection essentially consists in matters of precept,
for the primary precept is commanded without

measure: "Thou shalt love the Lord thy God with thy whole heart, and with thy whole soul, and with thy whole strength, and with thy whole mind; and thy neighbor as thyself." (Luke, 10:27.) Therefore, says St. Thomas, the perfection of charity falls under precept as a good that must be pursued.

There are grades of perfection. The minimum fulfillment of the precept of love, to which all are obliged, is to love nothing else more than God, contrary to Him, or equal to Him. There are degrees of perfection among those who fulfill this precept of charity. And, as we previously noted, there is a distinction between exterior perfection to which all are not held, and interior perfection to which all *are* held to the end.

The end of the Christian life, then, is perfection in charity, by fulfilling the primary precept of love of God and neighbor. The *necessary* means to this end (*ad esse*) are *the commandments* or *the secondary precepts;* but the observance of the counsels are useful, or better, means (*ad bene esse.*)

St. Thomas distinguishes a perfect from an imperfect observance of the precept of the love of neighbor, insofar as one assumes the needs of his neighbor as his own or simply refrains from doing to his neighbor what he would not want to have done to himself.[12] The imperfect observance of this precept, refraining from mortal sin and observing common justice, is, according to St. Thomas, the minimum requisite in the spiritual life. In another place, St. Thomas simply identifies imperfect observance with the keeping of the commandments and perfect observance with the additional acceptance of the counsels.[13]

While St. Jerome concluded that the rich young man of the Gospel lied in saying he had observed the secondary precepts from his youth, St. Chrysostom, whom St. Thomas follows, declares that the youth had truly observed all these things, but imperfectly. In proposing His counsels of perfection, Our Lord challenged him (and all, as we shall see) to a perfect observance of these precepts.

Precepts are given concerning acts of virtue. These acts can be either interior or exterior as both fall under precept, but in different ways. Interior acts pertain, in the strict sense, to purity of mind; moreover, all the virtues, moral as well as theological, are ordered to the love of God and of neighbor. The perfection of Christian life consists *essentially* in these interior acts. Hence with regard to these interior acts the counsels are ordained to the precepts as to an end. But the same is not true of exterior acts, which are greater in matters of counsel than in keeping the precepts. The perfection of Christian life consists *instrumentally* in the observance of the counsels, which are concerned with certain exterior acts by which this perfection is attained safely and easily. We can quote St. Thomas literally on this important point:

And so it is clear that the counsels are ordained to the precepts as to an end, insofar as they concern the *interior* acts of the virtues; but insofar as they concern *exterior* acts, the counsels are so ordained to the precepts that they may be kept surely and safely by removing impediments. And the first of these is the cause of the second, for the rigid observance of exterior acts is caused by the interior inclination of a soul that is well disposed.[14]

The counsels, then, in relation to the primary precept, and by way of adding certain exterior observances to the common observance of the secondary precepts, are instrumental and dispositive.[15] Hence, says St. Thomas, "the religious state was instituted principally for the pursuit of perfection through certain exercises by which impediments to perfect charity are removed."[16] St. Thomas describes the counsels as "instruments for attaining the perfection of charity,"[17] as "impulses to perfection and restraints from sins;"[18] observance of the counsels "prepares the way for a safer and more perfect observance of the devine precepts."[19]

It is important to see this position of the religious state as an integral part of the whole framework of the Christian life and pursuit of perfection. Religious vocation cannot be considered apart from the universal vocation to sanctification. And when it is considered, as it should be, as a dispositive and instrumental means to the unique end of perfection in charity, religious vocation will lose the hazy aura of "special-strange-something" which modern writers on the subject tend to give to it.

And in view of this assignment of religious vocation to its proper place in the direct line of salvation, which is the Christian vocation common to all, one will not be shocked (merely enlightened) by St. Thomas' enthusiastic insistence on inviting, even urging, all to consider, even try, the benfits of religious life. "For the religious," as one Thomist has succinctly put it, "makes a special vocation of the general vocation to sanctity . . . they are, so to speak, professional perfectionists." (Fr. J. M. Egan, O.P., "The Religious Vocation Today," *Integrity,* Oct., 1949, p. 31.)

Father Maggiolo (previously cited in the first chapter), following St. Thomas faithfully, speaks of religious vocation as "a normal thing in the Christian life," and deplores the tag of rarity given to it by contemporary authors. To show the position of the religious state in its relation to Christian perfection,

Father Maggiolo proposes a simple diagram, based on the teachings of St. Thomas, which we are incorporating here:

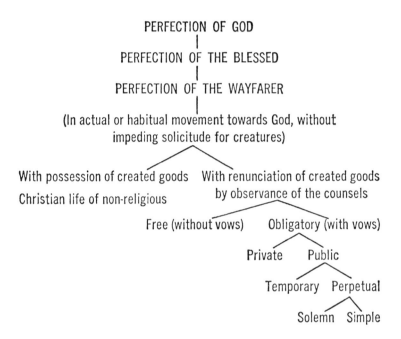

Recognizing this important inter-relationship, and realizing that religious life is in the direct line of salvation as a normal but better means of attaining the end of Christian life; i.e., that of partaking in the universal vocation to sanctification, we are ready to advance to St. Thomas' doctrine on the particular application of the evangelical counsels.

The point now is the question of just who are invited to the practice of the counsels, and, later on, how can they know that they are among the invited?

CHAPTER V

Who Are Invited?

Wₕₑₙ we see, as St. Thomas did, the proper place of the counsels in the plan of Christian perfection as useful means towards the fulfillment of the universal vocation to sanctification, we can understand why he differs so definitely from many modern writers in applying these counsels. His views on entrance into the religious life may shock those unfamiliar with the traditional treatment of this subject.

The Angelic Doctor praises anyone who can induce others to enter religion, unless violence, simony or deceit were involved.[20] He denies any need of long deliberation over the matter, because in itself the religious state is a better way of life. Nor, he says, should one seek advice about what we would call "having a vocation." The only time advice should be sought, St. Thomas counsels, is in matters of impediment (such as physical infirmity, debts etc.) or in the choice of a particular community. And even then, he warns, one should seek only the counsel of a person who will encourage rather than discourage the aspirant![21]

St. Thomas deplores the idea of preventing children, or those just emerging from a life of sin, or recent converts from seeking the advantages of the religious state. To ask them to wait and practice the precepts first, or to look for something exceptional in themselves, is, says St. Thomas, to misunderstand altogether the nature of the counsels.[22] Further, he strongly approves the practice of advising the religious state as a penance,[23] as well as praises making a private vow to enter religion at some time and then holding oneself to it.[24]

Surely this attitude towards entering the religious state greatly differs from that of many modern authors on the subject. They would advise a perfect practice of the precepts before attempting the counsels; they would advise the young to wait for maturity; they would advise the convert to become more settled in the practice of his new faith. Worst of all, they would imply the need for an introspective search for some special voice in the inmost depths of the soul. St. Thomas always approaches the subject from an objective aspect, and not from the unknown subjective aspect of an internal element—although he is the first to insist on a necessary divine movement and disposition. But for him this divine correlative to human aspiration would not be rare or exceptional.

Following his doctrine we can therefore propose a universal invitation to the practice of the particular counsels proposed by Our Lord. Who are invited to enter the religious state? All!

When St. Thomas, in his *Contra Retrahentes*, considered the particular problem of anxious deliberation over one's certainty of being called by God to enter the religious state, he specifically and distinctly proposed a universal objective vocation to the practice of the counsels. This treatment, his most particular application and approach to our contemporary problem, should be summarized as it is.[25] That he was talking about counsel in an absolute sense, as followed in the religious life, is unquestionable and obvious from the context.

Approaching the explicit counsel of Christ as revealed in Sacred Scripture, St. Thomas states the general principle that the words of Christ, as quoted and handed down to us in the Gospels, should be accepted as though we actually heard them from the mouth of Christ. He appeals to Scripture itself to substantiate this principle: "What I say to you, I say to all," (Mark 13:37) and "For whatever things have been written have been written for our instruction." (Rom. 15:4.)

Citing these texts and others, as well as a passage from St. Chrysostom, St. Thomas concludes that the words of Sacred Scripture were spoken not only to those present at the time of their oral transmission but also to all in the future who would read the revealed Word. But especially, says St. Thomas, let us see whether Our Lord's challenge to the rich youth applied to him alone or to all.[26] This important text in question, containing two of the counsels on which religious vows are based, is the response of Christ: "If thou wilt be perfect, go, sell what thou hast, and give to the poor, and thou shalt have treasure in heaven; and come, follow me." (Matt. 19: 21.)

Immediately St. Thomas calls the context of this passage to our attention. After the youth sadly went away, "for he had great possessions," Our Lord commented on the difficulty of the impediment of riches in the way of perfection, but reminded His disciples, and us, that "with God all things are possible." Then Peter reminded the Master that they had left all and followed Him, and he boldly asked what they would receive for their generosity. And then, says St. Thomas, Jesus *universally* promised a reward to all his intimate followers: "And everyone who has left house, or brothers, or sisters, or father, or mother, or wife, or children, or lands, for my name's sake, shall receive a hundredfold, and shall possess life everlasting." (Matt. 19:29.)

Therefore, says St. Thomas, the following of this counsel is directed to each one, no less than if Our Lord spoke to every Christian personally.[27] He cites St. Jerome and St. Chrysostom to verify the fact that the same counsel given to the rich young man is proposed to all. And so, he concludes very bluntly, the counsel given by Christ to this youth should be accepted as though it were given to all from the very mouth of Our Lord.[28]

Leaving the argument for universal vocation to religious life, according to this exegetical analysis in his *Contra Retrahentes,* we turn to what St. Thomas has to say about an important Scriptural difficulty to this thesis, one which appears in the enunciation of the counsel to virginity.

Previous to His encounter with the rich youth, Jesus had defended the indissolubility of marriage against the mundane mutterings of the pharisees, who found His saying difficult and even His disciples meditated aloud whether it might not be better to forego marriage entirely. Jesus told them of the eunuchs who had made themselves so for the kingdom of heaven's sake, saying: "Not all can accept this teaching, but those to whom it has been given . . . Let him accept it who can." (Matt. 19:11.) This seems to be a restriction, a qualification of Our Lord's later counsel of perfection to all, and an argument against universal religious vocation.

In his Scriptural commentaries, [29] St. Thomas explains the passage in this way: This counsel is given by God to those who ask for it and are willing to work for it. Not all take it because not all have the strength to abstain from marriage, not that any have such a strength of themselves, but by a gift of grace. It is not by natural power that this ability to accept this counsel arises; for if one depended on natural power alone, no one could take it. But, says St. Thomas, if this strength is from grace then *anyone can*; for Christ said: "Ask and it shall be given to you." (Luke 11:9) And so, he concludes, *by the grace of God all can take this counsel.*[30]

In treating this difficulty we are already anticipating the more pertinent problem of what is called *internal vocation*. The written or spoken Word of God cannot have efficacy without the grace of the Holy Spirit acting on the soul. This will be considered more thoroughly later on. For the present, it is sufficient to remind the reader that we have been on a purely objective plane in speaking of the universal vocation to the religious state. This is a matter of external, rather than internal, causality. The subjective, intrinsic and personal element is equally important;

for without divine light and movement urging the human response, universal religious vocation is a barren and sterile phrase. Yet it is important to observe the validity and value of the objective universality of the invitation to practice the counsels literally and absolutely, that is, in the religious state. For God is ready to give the grace of response to those who want it. And a generous soul, sincere in his intentions, can proceed unafraid.

Following St. Chrysostom, the Angelic Doctor says simply that not all can take this counsel because not everyone wants to. Although the reward is offered for heroic generosity, some seek only the glamor of such heroism without considering the sacrifice essential to it. Too many youngsters are immature in their understanding of religious life, seeing only superficial romance in such a vocation. Their expectant imagination pictures an heroic missionary riding into the sunset; they do not anticipate the hard work, loneliness and deprivations of such a life. (This is my own aside, and really belongs to the practical comments to be made later on.)

While *quibus datum est* (those to whom it is given) refers to the necessary help of grace, a gratuitous gift of God, yet this divine assistance will not be denied to those willing to do their part.[31] The dictum "Do your best and God will do the rest" surely applies to the aspirant timidly approaching the demands of religious life. What is required is a sincere disposition of will, as well as a clear understanding of what these demands are and how they can be met.

And lest anyone should think St. Thomas makes a singularly broad interpretation of this particular passage, we should point out immediately that he is following the unanimous interpretation of the Fathers, Doctors and early theologians of the Church. St. Jerome and St. Chrysostom, whom he cites, propose this interpretation. So does Bede, Euthymius, Theophylactus, Origen and others. St. Paul's wish, that all were in his state (I Cor. 7:7) indicates—as some point out—that this gift of continence is possible to many.[32]

The Jesuit commentator, Fr. C. A. Lapide, also adds St. Augustine to this list, as well as St. Ambrose and Tertullian, and he sums up the Patristic explanation in this way:

Here the evangelical counsel of celibacy is promulgated by Christ and proposed to all, counselled but not commanded. For St. Jerome and St. Chrysostom maintain that the words, "He that can take, let him take it," are the words of one exhorting and animating to celibacy. Moreover it is signified that as Christ gives this counsel, it is in our power to fulfill it, if we invoke the grace of God, and earnestly cooperate with it. Nor does the expression, 'He that can take,' do away with the force of this, for this only signifies that continence is a difficult thing. He who is willing to put a restraint on himself, who is willing to resist sensuality generously, who is willing to ascend the arduous peak of continence, let such a one embrace it, let him take it. (*Commentaria in Scripturam Sacram*, tom xv, *In Matth.*, c. xix, p. 424a.)

We cannot, of course, carry this point to the extreme of a kind of self-propulsion, so often implicitly, even at times explicitly, proposed by theologians who show more reckless enthusiasm than sound doctrine. For the Thomist, it goes without saying that one doesn't "ascend the arduous peak of continence" on his own will alone but, rather, is boosted up by the grace of God. Father Lagrange, for example, treads more carefully with cautious reservation. Speaking of this passage, he says: "At the same time He was even then inviting those to whom the inspiration would be given to imitate them; and if continence ever becomes a necessity in a particular case it is always made possible by prayer." (*The Gospel of Jesus Christ*, vol. 2, p. 92.)

St. Thomas, of course, is most insistent upon the necessary efficacious divine movement involved in anyone taking on any special aspect of the supernatural life; but that insistence is seen more often and more emphatically in other tracts. Hence the need of considering religious vocation in the context of his complete doctrine.

We have, perhaps, belabored the apparent Scriptural difficulty precisely because it does, at first sight, look ominous. But, clearly understood, this passage (about those to whom it is given taking or accepting) does not detract from the principle that the counsels, as proposed by Christ, are proposed to all.

Yet we cannot stop here, as many modern authors do, and say that that is all there is to religious vocation. God counsels all to the religious state. St. Thomas does not let it go at that. For, as a matter of record, God moves only some to respond to this invitation, not all. Obviously there is still much more to be understood about religious vocation in the whole context of theology. St. Thomas himself says, at this point, that there is still something else to be considered.[33] And here he distinguishes the *locutio*, or speaking, of Sacred Scripture from an interior speaking.

This sounds as though we are back where we started. But wait; such is not the case.

St. Thomas often uses this division of vocation into external and internal aspects when considering God's action upon man in matters pertaining to salvation. He employs this distinction in speaking of vocation to justification and in matters of faith and virtue.[34]

Again he applies this distinction in considering the direct calling of the Apostles.[35] In this instance he describes the interior *locutio* of God in this way: "To call interiorly is nothing other than to provide help to the human spirit when He wishes to convert us."[36]

While it is true that this divine assistance is necessary in religious vocation, as it is in every supernatural action, it seems improbable that in this passage he means to convey the usual correlative grace. There is something more profound and subtle in his terminology here, for he is making more of a distinction in this particular instance.

He says, for example, that this way in which God speaks interiorly is to be *preferred* to the exterior *locutio* of Sacred Scripture.[37] He refers to a definite speaking of the Holy Spirit, something more than the ordinary movement of grace in aiding the mind and will of man. Rather, this "speaking" seems to be a general reference to various manifestations of the work of the Holy Spirit in the soul. The light and motion of the Holy Spirit is present in every direct divine contact with the soul; but here St. Thomas seems concerned with its more manifest workings— not necessarily extraordinary in a marvellous sense, but at least in some way perceptible to the subject.

For St. Thomas says that if the exterior voice of God, in Sacred Scripture, is to be obeyed without delay, how much *more so* an interior speaking of God within the soul.[38] And again he separates these notions when he disparages delay in following Christ after an interior *or* an exterior vocation.[39] Father Garrigou-Lagrange, in applying this two-fold division to the vocation to infused contemplation does not insist on giving a full correlative sense to these terms, saying: "Generally the exterior vocation and the interior vocation are united . . ." (*Christian Perfection and Contemplation*, p. 338.) Thus he leaves room for a wider employment of these terms.

From these passages from St. Thomas, from the extraordinary examples he mentions, from a definitely different usage of the terms in other places— all these considerations make it clear that St. Thomas is speaking here of an aspirant who, to some degree, perceives a more insistent grace, a more perceptible movement of the Holy Spirit. And these degrees may vary, from the common experience of the youth who simply cannot get vocational ideas out of his mind even though unencouraged and occurring under unusual circumstances on up to the mystical vocational phenomena, such as the vision of the Blessed Mother counselling St. Albert the Great to enter the Order of Preachers and the dream of St. Catherine of Siena in which she was beckoned into the bark of St. Dominic.

St. Thomas always speaks of a universal vocation to the religious state from a purely objective point of view. He must, for in any particular case a candidate has to consider his personal disposition and situation and circumstances in relation to this objective norm. While it is true to say that Christ invites all to the better means of observing the precepts by practicing the counsels, the fact is, that God does move some to respond and others He does not. For in every inducement to the practice of the counsels "such a suggestion has no efficacy unless one is drawn interiorly by God . . . and so the religious resolve, by whomever it is suggested, is from God."[40] Jesus said: "No one can come to me unless the Father who sent me draw him." (John 6:44.) In any case, exterior or interior, whether the very challenge of Scripture incites or the Holy Spirit more directly inspires, God must move man to accept His invitation.

In God's plan there are other states of life and other offices to be filled. While the married state is not properly a state of perfection, nor equal to virginity in itself, yet for some particular person it will be his or her vocation, in the sense that in this state this individual passively executes the divine plan in his or her regard. Hence St. Thomas says that while universally it is said that virginity is better for a man than matrimony, the marital state may be better for some particular man.[41]

He mentions this subjective element in response to an objection that the same thing is not always expedient to all and therefore the counsels are not given to all. St. Thomas replies:

It should be said that the aforementioned counsels, *considered in themselves,* are expedient to all, but from the indisposition of some it may happen that to some they are not expedient because their dispositions are not inclined to such things. Hence Our Lord, in proposing the evangelical counsels, always makes mention of man's fitness for observing the counsels. For in giving the counsel of perpetual poverty (Matt. 19:21), He begins with the words, *If thou wilt be perfect,* and then He adds, *Go, sell what thou hast.* In like manner, when He gave the counsel of perpetual chastity, saying (Matt. 19:12): *There are eunuchs who have made themselves so for the kingdom of heaven's sake,* He immediately adds: *Let him accept it who can.* And again, the Apostle (I Cor. 7:35), after giving the counsel of virginity, says: *Now this I say for your benefit, not to put a halter upon you.*[42]

Hence, in proposing the universality of vocation to the practice of the evangelical counsels, St. Thomas is considering the counsels objectively, in themselves and not in relation to particular persons.

There is a subjective fitness, both natural and supernatural, which prepares a particular person to respond to this invitation. The New Law, as St.
Thomas reminds us, is primarily the very grace of
the Holy Spirit, which is given to the Christian faithful. The written Word contains only those things
which dispose or ordain the use of this grace.[43] Ordinarily, however, the movement of grace in religious
vocation is neither rare nor exceptional.

CHAPTER VI

Who Can Accept?

THE acceptance and undertaking of the evangelical counsels is the human response to the divine invitation. Granted that God invites all to use these better means to achieving Christian perfection in charity, the common vocation of all the faithful, the fact is that only some respond and enter the religious state. What is the nature of this response and how does God promote it?

With remarkable brevity, St. Thomas refers to this act of acceptance as *propositum religionis*, the simple resolve to enter religion, or the religious state.[44] This is an act of the will, a deliberate choice and resolution, consequent upon intellectual consideration of the object willed. While St. Thomas refers to this complicated human action with only two simple words, much is contained in this notion which requires thorough understanding.

Contemporary vocational terminology often includes such words as "desire" and "feels," implying definite sensible affections. Yet there is no influence upon the religious resolve which necessarily conjoins an emotional element. It may be there, but it doesn't have to be. One ordinarily does not feel grace, or the operation of the virtues, or the movement of the rational will. If a subject is sensibly affected in supernatural action this is accidental, a result of divine condescension of encouragement or consolation, or of the natural connection between the sensitive and rational powers.

Father Ortega, in a work previously cited,[45] calls this resolve to enter religion "a sincere and firm determination of the will, formed after mature deliberation." As for the element of feeling, he says: "This determination of the will to embrace the religious life can and commonly does have an overflow into sensible affection . . . but such a redundance is not necessary and the resolve to enter religious life, inspired by God, can exist even with sensible repugnance at the privations and practices of this same life."

Another aspect of vocational response, this one essential, requires consideration and concern. This really is a two-fold aspect, two sides to this and to every human action, separable only in speculation. I refer, of course, to the divine motion in human action, in all action. There is nothing which escapes the divine causality. As St. Thomas says, "Since God is the first universal cause, not of one genus only, but of all being, it is impossible for anything to occur outside the order of the divine government."[46] In all human action, then, God is the primary cause, man the secondary cause, and together they produce a single effect. (For all its importance, especially in establishing the Thomistic position in this matter of vocation, we cannot afford to go into an analysis of the Thomistic doctrine on premotion and grace, but must assume its acceptance in this discussion with only a few words of explanation.)

We must bear in mind, however, that God moves us so as not to interfere with our freedom. In fact, we are free only because God makes us so. Father Garrigou-Lagrange explains, simply but profoundly:

> This universal and immediate sway, exerted by providence, does not destroy, but safeguards the freedom of our actions. Not only does it safeguard liberty, but actuates it, for the precise reason that providence extends even to the free mode of our actions, which it produces in us with our co-operation; for this free mode in our choice, this indifference dominating our desire, is still within the realm of being, and nothing exists unless it be from God. (*Providence*, p. 160.)

Hence any resolve of the will has both a divine and human cause, producing within us a single voluntary effect. St. Thomas reprimands those who "seem to have drawn a distinction between that which flows from grace, and that which flows from free will, as if the same thing cannot come from both."[47] While St. Thomas does say, as we have noted, that this religious resolve cannot have efficacy unless it be from God, he likewise speaks of religious obligating themselves in the religious state of their own will—"*propria voluntate se obligant.*"[48]

God moves us, to be sure, but freely, according to our nature and not in violence against it. God tells us what to do, and moves us to do it, but in a way that remains wholly voluntary on our part. In showing that precept, prohibition, and counsel are effects of the divine will, peculiar to rational creatures, St. Thomas explains: "The rational creature is master of his own acts; and therefore concerning him certain special expressions of the divine will are assigned, inasmuch as God ordains rational creatures to act voluntarily and of themselves."[49]

Accepting the divine and human motion producing the human effect of religious resolve, we can now consider the principal supernatural and natural influences upon this *propositum religionis,* by which some accept God's invitation to serve in His household—the religious state.

Supernatural Influences

The necessity of grace in any salutary human action is evident in the context of theology. The exterior principles of man's supernatural action, as St. Thomas points out, are law and grace—"instructing us by law and helping us by grace."[50] He explicitly mentions this necessary divine enlightenment of the intellect and movement of the will in accepting the invitation to practice the evangelical counsels in the religious state.[51] Furthermore, St. Thomas refers to the movement of actual grace, as well as the form of sanctifying grace, as utterly free gifts which are in no way dependent upon man's action.[52] The Thomistic doctrine on grace is wholly opposed to that school of theologians who treat grace as a kind of common undetermined supernatural power which man can harness and steer into particular goals, such as the response to religious vocation.

An important question immediately arises. Is the grace involved in religious vocation special? The difficulty is to determine just what is meant by "special." Every actual grace is special in the sense that it moves this particular individual to this specifically good act. We must dismiss any consideration of the so-called *gratiae gratis datae* (apostolic graces, as distinguished from those given for personal sanctification), also of habitual or sanctifying grace (since this grace is rooted in the soul and not in the faculties as a proximate principle of action), and also any mystical phenomena (since we are concerned only with the ordinary process of religious vocation). Vocational graces might be called special in a very broad sense, in that their goal is an important and critical one which profoundly affects the recipient's eternal welfare.

But are these graces special in the sense that they are reserved for a few select souls or manifested in extraordinary ways? That those who receive such graces are thereby favored we must concede. But we say this in the same sense that we would speak of the mysterious predilection involved in predestination. The fact is that God wills antecedently that all men be saved and gives sufficient grace for this purpose. Yet consequently He efficaciously moves some to attain salvation. Salvation is a gratuitous gift of God granted to certain souls. Nevertheless, predestination is in God and we do not look for certain effects that can permit the faithful to be wholly passive in their vocation to salvation. We do not urge the faithful to "see if they are saved."

This analogy, of course, more than limps; it falls down altogether in the matter of obligation and fault. God does not oblige all to enter the religious state, nor is any fault, ordinarily, imputed to those who do not embrace it. Yet the similarity does exist with regard to the mystery of predilection and its consequences. God does invite all to practice the evangelical counsels. Yet all are not obligated to follow them. God moves some to accept his invitation freely and to choose this state of life.

So, only in a broad sense, therefore, is there a special gift involved in religious vocation. But we cannot discern these interior graces sufficiently to ask aspirants to look for them—in their "heart of hearts" or elsewhere. Even a recognition of grace through its effects, says St. Thomas, is imperfect knowledge.[53] We can look for certain indicative signs and canonically required qualities, but we should not call grace itself a vocation. For in such a broad sense we could call every grace the voice of God—"Today if you shall hear his voice, harden not your hearts." (Psalm 94, v.8.) Nor should the objective appeal to accept the challenge and follow the evangelical counsels be addressed to a select few. As with Christ, the exhortation should be made to all on the basis of manifest sincerity.

Ordinarily the grace influencing the response to religious vocation is not uncommon, rare or extraordinary, but within the ordinary economy of salvation. Otherwise St. Thomas would not have been so enthusiastically insistent on encouraging all to enter the religious state; nor would he have presupposed such future grace coming to children placed in convents or monasteries, who were not yet able to make a mature resolve and advance to vows. Nor does the Church, in her legislation and practice, seek any extraordinary supernatural gift in those who seek admission into the religious state. Only an unwitting, and untheological, counsellor would advise an aspirant to search within himself for some special sign.

Furthermore, the very relation of counsel to precept and perfection, as shown, opposes any notion of some uncommon, reserved or extraordinary grace in religious vocation. The sincere disposition of the faithful Christian, cooperating with the daily graces offered him, can prepare for that series of graces which culminate in the vows of religion. While the gift of perseverance in the religious state is likewise a gift from God, it is the ordinary fulfillment of all that has preceded if the religious does not oppose the graces of his state. Father Ortega, commenting on St. Thomas on this point,[54] says: "Every faithful Christian is fit to undertake and fulfill these vows, because Our Lord Who has counselled them to all will deny to none the grace to fullfill them." This statement should be modified a bit, because some are impeded from entering religion and others are ill-disposed. But granting the lack of prohibitive impediments and the presence of a sincere disposition, surely the grace of fulfillment and perseverance will not be lacking. More about the so-called "lost vocation" later on.

Now we should consider the influence exercised by the infused virtues which flow from habitual grace. Response to religious vocation is a good act, and every good act pertains to virtue.[55] Moreover, the element of perseverance in the intention to enter religious life over a period of time indicates the need for a habit—a virtue or virtues—which will bring about the necessary actions required in the complete response to religious vocation.

In some respect, of course, all of the theological virtues and many of the moral virtues are exercised in producing and preserving the acceptance of the invitation to the religious state. Faith illumines the mind in the consideration of the goal of religious life; hope encourages with its divine promises of help and reward; charity inflames the soul to seek such salutary means of union with God. Prudence discerns the counsels as the best means of attaining the goal of life, for "a man is said to be prudent who orders well his acts towards the end of life."[56]

One could go on through many of the moral virtues influencing the acceptance of God's invitation to practice the evangelical counsels; but one particular virtue, as St. Thomas points out, is prominent and proximate, and it even imposes the very name of the state and vocation of which we speak: "Religion is a virtue whereby a man offers something to the service and worship of God . . . wherefore those are called religious who give themselves up entirely to the divine service.[57]

The vows pertain to religion as an exterior act of that virtue.[58] And from this end, or fulfillment, of religious vocation we can recognize the principal virtue influencing its beginning; for the means are proportioned to the end to which they are ordained. The virtue of religion has as its object reverence for the divine excellence and subjection to the divine principality.[59] This comprises the religious debt man owes to God, a debt impossible to pay in strict justice. Man makes his greatest effort to pay by totally giving himself through the vows of religious life, thus most perfectly practicing the virtue of religion, which is the greatest of the moral virtues because it is concerned with those things that are immediately ordained to the honor of God.[60]

Immediately and intimately connected with religious vows, the goal of religious vocation, is the principal and universal act of the virtue of religion, namely the act of devotion. The very word "devotion" is derived from *vovere,* to vow.[61] Generally, the virtue of religion, with its interior act of devotion, is a directing virtue and imperates the acts of other virtues, directing them to the worship and service of God.[62] Hence by religious devotion we offer whatever we do to God, making all of our actions, in a sense, worshipful.

Particularly, in religious vocation, the virtue of religion through an intense act of devotion effects the act of will (*propositum religionis*) in man's acceptance of God's invitation. For "devotion is the act of the will by which man offers himself to God to serve Him Who is the ultimate end."[63] Fr. Walter Farrell, O.P., in an article entitled "Virtues of the Household," published in *The Thomist* (July, 1946), concludes that "this act of devotion in its highest degree is what we mean by the human side of religious vocation."

The gifts of the Holy Ghost also influence the religious resolve, facilitating the will to docility. The gifts, like charity to which they are related, admit of gradation. The first of these grades is ordered to the fulfillment of the precepts, the second to the fulfillment of the counsels and the third to the execution of heroic acts.[64]

The gift of Piety, working with matters pertaining to divine worship, may facilitate the total dedication to divine worship, which is the goal of religious vocation.[65] But the reverential subjection to God, proper to the virture of religion, is directly connected with the gift of Fear of the Lord. For it is this filial fear of losing the paternal love of God that provokes man's flight from irreligion to the due service and proper worship of God.[66]

The religious is a professional perfectionist in this fearful pursuit, devoting himself wholly and entirely to divine service and worship. Stripped of both external and internal possessions, the religious is blessed because of his utter poverty of spirit—that is, a poverty of spiritual impediments to his reverential subjection to God and the perfect ordering of his life. This gift of Fear of the Lord is directed by the intellectual gift of Widsom, for it is only by a share in divine vision, that we can recognize this perfect ordering of life.

Perhaps the most apparent aspect of religious consecration is the difficult sacrifice demanded of one who would assume this rich spiritual poverty. Such sacrifice obviously takes courage, fortitude, in the face of hardship. Thus the virtue of Fortitude in all its parts, particularly magnanimity and magnificence, must urge the hesitating steps into the cloister. The small-minded, engrossed in petty pursuits, are not disposed for religious life. The religious dares to undertake great things for God, trusting in

His movement to achieve them. Bringing a divine mode of mobility, the gift of Fortitude will boost the generous man who dares to climb beyond the rung of reason in his ambition.[67]

The intellectual gift of Counsel will guide this power of fortitude. At the same time, Counsel will perfect the prudence of the choice of religious life as the most perfect means to fulfill the Christian vocation and face the finality of religious dedication.[68] Aided by this gift of Counsel, the generous and courageous soul resolving to enter religious life will do so with tranquil and secure conviction—with the unruffled serenity of a fool for Christ.

Natural Influences

A questionnaire asking religious what influenced their vocations would elicit replies as unusual as they would be varied. And perhaps nothing that we have mentioned up to this point would be included specifically in their answers. For the workings of the Holy Spirit within us are taken for granted, a remembered lesson in the catechism. At any rate, these workings cannot be very well described as a personal experience. Rather, recollections of vocational influences would be particular remembrance of incidents and circumstances which, in a broad sense, might be termed external graces.

Everything that happens is within God's providence and sometimes He uses the negative influences of the world, as well as positive inspirations (words of a sermon, a retreat conference), as occasions for conversion of life. Natural circumstances, occasions, environment, temperaments, talents, example, advice—all play a part in influencing the resolve to enter religious life. For, as St. Thomas says, "those whom God chooses for something, He prepares and disposes so that they will be found fit for that for which they are selected."[69]

The circumstances which influence the turning of mind and heart to the total service of God are familiar and personal experiences known to every religious. Each one's gratitude for that odd and peculiar incident was long ago expressed by St. Paul: "In every circumstance give thanks, for this is God's will for you in Christ Jesus." (I Thess. 5:18.) Most important of all personal influences will be that of the family, the environment of the Christian home. In almost every instance, as a matter of recorded investigation, the generous response to religious vocation comes from an individual favored by the ideal surroundings and compelling influence of an exemplary Catholic family. Pope Pius XI, in his encyclical on the priesthood, says: "To this ordinary rule of Divine Providence exceptions are rare and only serve to prove the rule." The good example also of teaching Sisters and Brothers, or other religious known to the aspirant, strongly influence his or her resolve to join their ranks.

Needless to say, the very living of a good Catholic life in itself often brings that series of graces which lead to total religious dedication. The advice of others also exerts a strong influence, either encouraging or impeding the response to the divine invitation. St. Thomas, so convinced of the advantages of religious life and so lacking in the cautious hesitancy of contemporary writers on the subject, devoted a separate article in his *Summa Theologica* to the praise of those who encourage others to enter the religious state.[70]

When asked whether one should seek much advice and spend a long time deliberating over entering religion, he answered in the negative. For, of itself, entering religion is a better good to perform and we deliberate only over questionable goods! As for the aspirant, he need not worry about his ability to fulfill the obligations of religious life because he will trust not in himself, but in divine help. Finally, St. Thomas says, one needs advice only if a grave impediment stands in the way, or if the aspirant is undecided as to where and how to enter. And in such a case, he says, one should consult only those who will not prevent his entrance.[71] Certainly St. Thomas showed no concern for a search for some-special-something.

Anyone familiar with the life of St. Thomas, and knowing his experience of family opposition to his vocation, will understand his almost bitter estimation of family advice in such matters. He remarks that if advice is necessary, stay away from worldly people, "among whom the wisdom of God is considered foolishness"; and family or relatives who "in this proposal are not friends but enemies." "In this case," he says, "the advice of family or relatives especially should be avoided."[72] This passage should be read in the context of his time and his own experience; but today, unfortunately, many aspirants to religious life, particularly among women, face their fiercest opposition from their own families.

A casual reader might suspect personal prejudice in the passage. If so, he should consult some of the Fathers of the Church on this point, especially St. Jerome and St. Bernard, or Pope Pius XI in the encyclical cited—or, for that matter, any priest who has met the problem of objecting parents. St. Alphonsus does not hesitate to teach that anyone, and especially parents, who impede a religious vocation, even by mere persuasion or promises, commits a grave sin.

We have already mentioned the condition of suitability that St. Thomas considered in his treatment of counsel. In that instance St. Thomas might have been concerned with the whole subjective side of religious vocation, including all the influences affecting the response under divine providence. He also specifically mentions inclination and temperament as factors influencing a choice of life. He says:

Human nature generally inclines towards various acts and offices . . . But because it works out differently in different people, insofar as it is individualized in one or another, it inclines one subject more to one of these offices, and another subject more to another, according to the difference of temperament in individuals. And it is owing to this difference, as well as to divine providence, which governs all, that one person chooses one position in life, agriculture, for example, and another person another job. And so it is too that some choose the married life and some the contemplative.[73]

Yet this suitability, or aptitude, cannot be considered as the sole determinant or taken on purely natural grounds. Religious life, unlike secular professions, is not based on natural qualities or adaptability. The transforming power of grace is a necessary part of the picture, and sometimes the very kinks and quirks of personality which suggest unsuitability can, and perhaps should, be ironed out in the daily presses of community life. If not before, judgment can be made in the trial of the novitiate.

We have indicated only a few of the factors which influence the resolve to enter the religious state. These are not comprehensive but may help us to discover who can accept the divine invitation. Each case, however, must be judged in all its subjectiveness by the proper spiritual director or religious superior.

CHAPTER VII

Some Confirmations

THE position of St. Thomas, proposing and even insisting on an objective general invitation to the practice of the evangelical counsels in the religious state, is confirmed by the unanimous opinion of the Fathers of the Church.

Among the Greek Fathers, particular references can be found in the works of Saints Basil, Gregory Nazianzen and John Chrysostom. Western Fathers explicitly approving the general nature of the objective call to the counsels, include Saints Ambrose, Jerome and Augustine.

St. Ambrose said: "There are eunuchs who have made themselves so for the kingdom of heaven . . . while this is not commanded to all, yet all are invited."

St. Jerome does not hesitate to urge an aspirant, Heliodorus, to overcome all obstacles to his intention to adopt the monastic life, saying: "If your father should prostrate himself before you at the door, step over him and go on . . . In this case the only way

for you to show your affection for your father is to
be cruel to him."

When St. Augustine was asked what would happen to the human race if everyone were to practice
the counsels, he blandly replied: "The City of God
would be filled the sooner, and the end of the world
hastened."

Some theological writers, both in the early Church
and more recently, have considered the moral obligation of some to enter the religious state. This attitude was stimulated by commentators on passages
of Scripture which seemed to indicate dire consequences following a rejection of the invitation to follow Christ through the practice of the counsels. In
the key passage, the story of the rich young man, the
youth goes away sad, manifesting a disturbed conscience, and Our Lord projects a dismal future for
anyone so attached to worldly possessions.* Other
passages (Luke, 9:57 and Matt., 8:19) show a need
for urgency in responding to a call from Christ; there
is not even time to bury a father or say goodbye to
the folks at home. The parable of the discourteous
guests invited to the banquet (Luke, 14:15 and
Matt., 22:1) can be, and was, appropriated to the
invitation to religious life. But most theologians today agree that the counsels can oblige gravely only
those who receive this invitation in a certain and ex-

---

* *Matthew* 19:21-24 and *Luke* 18:18-25. —*Publisher*, 2005.

traordinary manner or, because of personal dispositions, require a life of permanent penance to achieve
salvation.

Anyway, the general nature of the objective invitation to practice the counsels is held unanimously
by the Fathers of the Church. But, St. Thomas himself says, "The practice of the Church, which should
be observed always and in all instances, has the
greatest authority. Therefore it is better to adhere to
the practice of the Church rather than to the authority of an Augustine, a Jerome, or any other doctor."[74]

The practice of the Church in this matter can be
recognized in the formulation of her canon law, gov-
erning the moral life of her members. While a whole
section of this code of law is concerned with the religious state, only a single canon has reference to the
entrance of candidates to that state in which the
evangelical counsels are practiced. Without even using the term "vocation," the Church simply says:
"Any Catholic, who is free from legal impediments,
has the right intention, and is capable of bearing the
burdens of the religious life, can be admitted into a
religious organization." (Canon 538.)*

The simple phrase "any Catholic" implicitly approves the doctrine of the universality of the invitation, in itself, to the religious state of life. Because
the literal practice of the evangelical counsels is ac-

---

* The author is referencing the 1917 Code of Canon Law, which
was in effect until the new Code was promulgated in 1983.
                                        —*Publisher*, 2005.

complished in a public state of religious life, it falls under the external jurisdiction of the Church, who admits to it only her own members. The Church further exercises her jurisdiction by naming particular impediments to such a public practice of these counsels.

Impediments to valid admission into a religious community are listed in the first paragraph of Canon 542. The following persons cannot be admitted *validly* to the novitiate: (1) Catholics who voluntarily have joined a non-Catholic or atheistic sect— This does not apply to converts to the Catholic faith. (2) Those who have not completed their fifteenth year. (3) Those who enter religion under the influence of violence, grave fear, or fraud—concealing, for example, a prohibitive condition or personal health or family situation. (4) Married persons, as long as the marriage bond lasts. From this impediment the Holy See does dispense, but only rarely and in the case of elderly persons mutually consenting to such a petition. (5) Those who are, or have been, bound by the vows of religious profession— either in the same or another institute. (6) Those who are liable to punishment because they have committed a grave crime, of which they have been or can be accused. (7) A bishop, residential or titular, even though nominated and not yet consecrated.

(8) Clerics who are actually bound by oath to the service of a diocese or the missions.

In the second paragraph of the same canon, the Church lists impediments to *licit* admission to the religious state. Though their admission would be *valid*, it is *unlawful* to admit to the novitate: (1) Clerics in sacred orders, without consulting the local Ordinary or against his manifest will. (2) Persons who are in debt and insolvent. (3) Persons charged with the administration of temporal affairs, which might cause the institute to be involved in lawsuits or other difficulties. (4) Those who are obliged to support their parents, or grandparents, who are in grave need. (5) Those who in religion would be destined for the priesthood, from which they would be prohibited by an irregularity or other canonical impediment. (6) Those who belong to an Oriental rite may not enter an institute of the Latin rite without the written permission of the Sacred Congregation of the Oriental Church. (7) Those who have left a seminary. (This impediment is of recent origin and is contained in a decree issued jointly by the Sacred Congregation of Religious and the Sacred Congregation of Seminaries and Universities, July 25, 1941.)

The Holy See alone can dispense from these impediments. Besides these canonical impediments, individual institutes may make specific requirements of their own. The absence of these requirements in a candidate constitutes an impediment, from which the superior general of a pontifical institute can usually dispense with the approval or advice of his council. In diocesan congregations the local Ordinary can grant dispensations from impediments contained in the constitutions, since he first approved them.

In the case of minors seeking admission to a novitiate the Code of Canon Law does not require the consent of parents but merely demands completion of minimum age of fifteen years. Charity and obedience, however, may dictate a reasonable delay required by parents, at least until the candidate is of responsible age according to civil law. The superior or advisor must exercise prudence in considering parental objections.

This is all that the Church in her Canon Law has to say about impediments to entering the religious state. This, of course, is a minimum legal view as far as the Church is concerned; she ordinarily respects the right of the superiors of institutes to accept or reject candidates according to their own discretion.

So far, the practice of the Church from a legal point of view is perfectly clear and specific. Note, however, that in the original canon two other qualities are required in the candidate for religious life—"moved by a right intention and fitted to bear the burdens of this life." Here the focus is on subjective dispositions. Objectively, any Catholic free from specific impediments can enter religious life. But subjectively, and much more difficult to determine, personal qualities of mind and will, along with affective and physical dispositions, are necessary. There is wide latitude here for discussion, but it is more pertinent to the next chapter's consideration of restrictions or reservations.

The difficulty is not so much in the determination of what a right intention is but in the judgment of whether or not this particular candidate has it. Essentially what is required is a sincere and deliberate resolve to seek perfection in charity through the religious state of life, according to the rule and constitutions of a certain religious institute. In other words, in St. Thomas' terms, a right *propositum religionis*.

It is not easy to determine the presence, or absence, of such an intention in another. "For who among men knows the things of a man save the spirit of the man which is in him?" (I Cor., 2:11.) And even one's own judgment can be incorrect. We may not only deceive others but also, and perhaps more easily, ourselves.

Hence a true understanding of the nature, especially the sacrifices, of the religious state is necessary, along with an unconditional and unwavering will to use the means provided which are necessary to obtain the end of religious life.

Cardinal Cajetan, commenting on St. Thomas' teaching that one need not doubt his own strength to undertake the rigors of religious life, because that strength comes from divine assistance, says that we should diligently observe here that the absence of any impediment and the presence of a right disposition are presupposed. And, he says, honestly placing his trust in God to sustain him in the religious state and doing what he can to fulfill its observances.

The importance of a right intention, a proper religious resolve, can not be over-emphasized. Yet it does not matter whence this proposal arises. Even if it comes from the devil, says St. Thomas, it is a good thing, ultimately from God, and should be carried out.[75] For everything good is from God and, in any case, such an intention will not have efficacy without the grace of God. And so it is possible for someone to enter religion without a right intention, even without knowing it, and then acquire a true and firm resolve after entrance. The opposite intentional process, of course, is also possible. And this affects the so-called "lost vocation"; but more about that later.

The legal qualifications for entrance include, finally, a fitness to bear the burdens of religious life. Here again the constituted authority, the superior of the institute, must exercise a prudent judgment. The physical fitness of the candidate must be proportionate to the demands and hardships ordinarily encountered by members of the chosen community. Certain physical conditions which are chronic immediately disqualify the candidate, lest he or she be a burden instead of an asset to the community.

Moral fitness does not mean an attainment of perfection before entrance, for this is the very purpose of religious life. One doesn't enter the religious state because he is holy but because he wants to become holy. This point may seem labored and unnecessary; but, as a matter of fact, the young and idealistic candidate may feel unfit because of his recognition of moral defects. Nor is moral fitness required in the same degree for entering religion as it is for preparing for the priesthood, since the religious state in itself is a state of penance. What is required is a sincere will, manifested by honest effort and an earnest use of the salutary means provided in religious life. On the other hand, superiors must safeguard the community and its reputation. Hence habitual moral deviates or public sinners or known criminals are not considered fit subjects for the religious state.

So much for the few legal requirements imposed by the Church on candidates for religious life. Note that the word "vocation" is not used and that the Church restricts the general invitation to the religious state only in external matters. Latitude is given to spiritual directors and religious superiors in judging the internal dispositions of the candidate to determine the presence or absence of "a right intention" and fitness "to bear the burdens of religious life."

The Church officially manifests her mind in the matter of vocation in other ways. Because of the responsibilities of the priest as an *alter Christus* in the world and an instrument of God in the dispensation of the fruits of the Redemption for the salvation of souls, the Church expresses more concern over sacerdotal vocation than vocation to the religious state.

There is a marked difference between these two, and the difference must be borne in mind. Primarily, the priesthood is for others, to provide for the supernatural life of souls under the ministry of the particular priest; whereas the religious state primarily is for one's own sake to provide for the individual religious in his pursuit of perfection in charity. Secondarily, of course, these benefits redound to others through apostolic contact, either by prayer or by personal encounter in the work of the Church.

Hence in the divine governance, the execution of God's providence, priests are men who are singled out and fitted by nature and grace to play significant roles in the continuing drama of the Redemption of Christ. Divine vocation to the priesthood, then, and the graces consequent upon it, are special because all are not so called and prepared. The Church, in her official language, does employ the word "vocation" when speaking of those intended for sacred orders.

You will recall the vocational controversy which occurred among theologians in France in the early part of this century, which was described in the second chapter of this book. When followers of the attraction theory were opposed by the writings of Canon Lahitton they demanded that these writings be examined by proper authorities in Rome. As we pointed out earlier, the works of Canon Lahitton were not condemned, but this did not mean that the oversimplification of Lahitton's theory was approved either. What is important is the specific reply given on this question of vocation, and although the response primarily concerned sacerdotal vocation, I think an *a pari* argument for applying these principles is justified. The decree of the Roman Commission examining the works of Canon Lahitton has parallel significance in the study of the nature of religious vocation. This decision was contained in a letter from the Cardinal Secretary of State to the Bishop of Aire, and was later confirmed in official form by Pope Pius XI*(Cf. *Acta Apostolicae Sedis,* IV, 1912, p. 485; V, 1913, p. 290.)

Let us summarize the principal points of this decision with regard to sacerdotal vocation and see their parallel application to religious vocation:

1. No one has a right to ordination antecedent to the free choice of the bishop. (No one has a right to religious profession antecedent to the acceptance into a community by a legitimate superior.)

2. The requisite on the part of the ordained, called sacerdotal vocation, does not consist, necessarily and ordinarily, in certain attractions of the subject or inducements of the Holy Spirit. (No sensible attraction is necessary in the aspirant to the religious state, nor any unusual or extraordinary manifestation of the Holy Spirit.)

3. Nothing more is necessary in the subject than a right intention and suitability, founded upon the gifts of nature and grace, giving reasonable assur-

---

* The author apparently means not Pope Pius XI, but rather Pope St. Pius X (reigned 1903-1914). —*Publisher*, 2005.

ance that the candidate can fulfill the duties and obligations of the sacerdotal state. (The only requisite needed in the aspirant to religious life is a right intention, (*propositum religionis,* in the terms of St. Thomas), founded upon natural and supernatural dispositions evident enough to indicate a fitness to fulfill the duties and obligations of this state of life.)

These parallel requisites serve as another confirmation of the Thomistic position on the nature of religious vocation. The attraction theory is untenable when applied either to the priesthood or the religious state. So also is the theory, expressed by Canon Lahitton and his followers, which confuses ecclesiastical vocation with divine vocation. Ordination or acceptance to vows is called "ecclesiastical" vocation. In some degree this admittance by Church authorities to orders or vows confirms externally the internal rightness of dispositions in the candidate. But the coincidence of ecclesiastical and divine vocation is not always certain because a human defect of judgment may be involved.

Aspirants to the priesthood and to the religious life like to think that ordaining bishops and accepting religious superiors, officially representing Christ on earth, insure the presence of divine vocation by admitting the candidate to orders or to vows. But, as a matter of fact, admittance to ordination or profession does not guarantee that a candidate is responding to a divine vocation.

Pronouncement of vows is a public act of worship, but the very act of the vow is essentially internal and personal. Ecclesiastical authority has power over the former in the external forum but not the latter, which belongs to the internal forum and is a free matter between God and the individual soul. Only a human judgment, with no more than moral certitude, can ascertain and assert a divine design in human behavior. Delegated authority within the Church can err in applying juridical power. It is difficult to judge a right intention and personal fitness in so profound a matter. Proper authority must so judge, but its judgment in such matters is not infallible.

Speaking of the priesthood, Pope Pius XI, in his encyclical on the subject, speaks of "those who accept ordination through human respect, without vocation and without the priestly spirit." Cardinal Gasparri, a most eminent canonist, distinguishes a divine from an ecclesiastical vocation and points out that the latter is not absolute and does not take away the important element of free will in the subject. Further, in the same commentary, he declares that some can receive sacred orders who lack a divine vocation*and these, he says, are guilty of mortal sin and their apostolate will not be fruitful but injurious to souls.

We are, of course, mixing our matter here because our concern is with religious rather than sacerdotal vocation. We should settle what is validly an *a pari* conclusion with reference to the religious state. The glaring defect in this fusion of matter is that vocation to the priesthood is definitely a special vocation, restricted to select souls; whereas religious life is not restricted to a chosen few, with any judgment against those who enter without some kind of reserved invitation. Nevertheless the original distinction is preserved and can be applied to both sacerdotal and religious candidates. For divine vocation, in either case, is of God and affects the internal forum; whereas ecclesiastical vocation is of man and concerns only the external forum, the public practice of the Church.

The principal difficulty is in determining the presence or absence of a right intention, and then judging personal fitness. Right intention and character are internal factors; we can only observe external behavior as an expression of man's spiritual nature. Deliberately or not, the true mind and habits of will in a man can be covered and remain hidden. They can be ascertained with no more than moral

---

* To "lack a divine vocation," although ordained, would evidently mean to lack a right intention or personal fitness for the priesthood.
—*Publisher*, 2005.

certitude, even by competent ecclesiastical superiors. That certitude, however, joins strength and assurance when residing in proper authority, in those who have the grace of office to make such judgments which so strongly affect the good of the Church. Thus the accepted candidate has reason to be assured of the rightness of his action insofar as he can, excepting always a direct divine revelation.

Certain practices within the Church, especially the early Church, confirm the Thomistic doctrine on the objective nature of Christ's invitation to the faithful to the practice of the evangelical counsels. In the Church of the Middle Ages, for example, it was not uncommon for parents to offer very young children to the religious life by placing them in convents and monasteries at an early age. The obvious presumption was that upon reaching maturity these youngsters would want to make profession of vows and God would provide the necessary grace to prompt such a supernatural resolve. The implication is equally obvious: that such a course did not demand any extraordinary divine selection for this state of life. And the Church approved this practice. St. Benedict was such a case; so was St. Thomas himself, although he chose a different order from that in which he was placed for education as a child.

Another common practice in the early Church was to advise notorious sinners to assume the penitential life of the religious state. Sometimes this was only a prolonged retreat, without vows and actual membership in the religious community. But frequently counsel was given to penitents to make formal entrance into the convent or monastery. This counsel could hardly be given if much consideration was necessary to determine whether or not one "had a vocation" to this state of life.

An opposite practice of the Church, confirming our position, is the counsel given to those especially gifted and favored by God to retire to convent life. This was done in the cases of both Bernadette of Lourdes and Lucy of Fatima. I am not implying a lack of free choice in either saint or sinner who is advised to enter the religious state of life and does so. They are and must be free, and not forced, to enter the cloister. But the evident implication is that no extraordinary sign of special vocation is required in order to counsel a candidate to the religious state to adopt it. Rather, the presumption is in favor of a general invitation to try such a life, with the assurance of the necessary grace to persevere.

Finally, the Church's approbation of Thomistic doctrine includes the theology of vocation which the

Angelic Doctor proposes. "Go to Thomas," the Vicar of Christ has advised, and this we have done in our attempt to dissolve the unnecessary mystery and consequent confusion which becloud our popular notion of religious vocation.

CHAPTER VIII

And Some Reservations

In what we have said so far there is an obvious danger of oversimplification: some reservations, or qualifications are very much in order. Without them we would be guilty, if only by implication, of denying two necessary mysteries; one supernatural and the other natural. Our purpose is to dispel only the unnecessary mystery.

Divine vocation is essentially a supernatural mystery, because it consists in divine decrees executed by God's governance over our lives. As we pointed out earlier, to know one's vocation absolutely would be to know God's will, and therefore God Himself, directly. Our natural mode of knowledge, even when enlightened by divine revelation and the supernatural gifts, can discern only the effects of divine vocation in a particular person, and this, as we have said, can provide only moral certitude of the direction God intends for the individual.

As Jacques Maritain once wrote: "Vocation is a supernatural mystery. Every natural explanation which may be offered relates only to accidentals, trivial in comparison with the essential motive." (*The Angelic Doctor,* p. 3.) Nevertheless, only through such comparatively trivial accidentals can we make the moral judgment necessary to encourage or discourage the aspirant to religious life. The danger, we repeat, is to emphasize the essential mystery which defies successful exploration.

And while we, along with St. Thomas, emphasize the objective general invitation to the practice of the evangelical counsels, we are the last to forget or ignore the necessary efficacy of God's grace in achieving any supernatural merit whatsoever. But St. Thomas himself takes for granted our recognition of the facts of the profound mysteries of predestination, premotion and predisposition. The difficulty is that there is nothing we can do to attain a comprehension of these divine elements in vocation; otherwise they would not be mysteries. Yet we can, and should, examine the observable effects of this divine action on the human personality and act, or direct, accordingly.

The natural mystery involved here is the complex individual personality of every subject responding to this, or any other, invitation which affects the course of any particular human history.

It's all very well to propose an accurate metaphysical definition of man and say that he is "a rational animal," or learn from the catechism that he is "a creature of God, composed of body and soul." These are abstract concepts applicable to any and every man. They do not, of course, describe the complex personality of this particular person. All men are *created* equal,* but they are not *born* equal, nor do they mature in the same environment and under the same circumstances. We all possess the same human nature; yet everyone possesses an individual, and different, personality. Every man, therefore, is an individual mystery in himself by the natural constitution of his personality.

Differences in personality are not merely acquired through environment and experience. There are natural potentialities which will distinguish a personality from birth; each one is disposed differently to encounter the vicissitudes of his life and produce his own personal history.

Innate psychic factors influencing the individuation of personality are mental and volitional dispositions which predispose a person for certain intellectual and moral potentialities and inclinations. By our attempts to measure natural intellectual aptitude, apart from achievement tests, we demonstrate our acceptance of innate differences of cognitional ability in individuals. Experience also shows a nat-

---

* That is, all men are equally human. —*Publisher*, 2005.

ural difference in a person's intellectual bent towards either speculative or practical aptitudes. Artistic talent is a more particularized manifestation of a connatural aptitude of the practical intellect. Furthermore, theologians and directors of souls express appreciation of natural volitional tendencies in persons, inclining one to cultivate more easily this virtue or this vice.

Physically, from birth, we are differentiated by sex, which has profound effects, psychological as well as physiological, on the personality. Body-build, or somatic type, and physiological disposition, especially in the endocrine glandular system, also affect one's appearance and the affective tone of a personality. Temperament, characteristic emotional reaction, is rooted in the constitution of the endocrine, or ductless, glands. Hence the traditional types of melancholic, choleric, sanguine and phlegmatic temperaments have a natural and innate foundation, although they can be modified by acquired habits of behavior.

At this point we have indicated multiple differences which predispose the individual personality before the course of a human life has begun.

Acquired influences which individuate personality are even more extensive. Environment, especially in the broad sense extending beyond a particular geographical position, exerts strong pressures. Experience forms the pattern of encounter, action and reaction. Education, in the home and school and church, develops the impetus of motivation.

No one of these hereditary dispositions or acquired attitudes determines the personality, nor do all of them together produce the complex of an individual person. Personality is not the sum of these elements but the inter-play of all under the central direction of man's will, which is inviolably free.

Above this natural composite of human personality, the autonomous action of the will is influenced by the divine action of grace, a supernatural enlightenment and movement which prompts all that we do, and can develop habits of virtue to form a good character. The rejection of sanctifying grace reduces the personality to a natural level;* the habitual deflection of actual graces leaves us to the development of habits of vice and produces a bad character. Character is the moral part of personality, shaped by habits of will, which is subject to grace.

This summary of dynamic psychology, with the addition of pertinent theological principles, should provide us with an appreciation of the complexity, and therefore mystery, of human personality.

Just as St. Thomas presupposes an awareness of the supernatural mystery of divine vocation, he also

---

* The "natural level" is actually a theoretical construct which does not exist in reality in human life. Every person past the age of reason is either in the state of grace or in the state of mortal sin.
—*Publisher*, 2005.

presumes our realization of the natural mystery, by reason of complexity, of the human subject of vocation. Cardinal Cajetan was careful to point out, when commenting on St. Thomas' stress on the general invitation to practice the counsels, that the Angelic Doctor presumed a right intention in the subject. We might add here that he also presumes the fitness or suitability of the subject. And since one's intention can be changed more easily than one's personality make-up, this note of fitness or aptitude is a more important reservation to the general thesis of a universal invitation to religious life.

Even St. Thomas' stand in favor of admitting habitual sinners, converts and children to the religious state must be qualified in order to be understood. He is speaking abstractly, not in reference to particular people, and ideally, without reference to prohibitive conditions. He presumes in the former sinner a will fixed sufficiently to break bad habits of the past. In the convert he is speaking of one embracing Christianity as a unified faith, without the need for the kind of re-education and re-orientation required in the contemporary convert from Protestant faith, tradition, environment and psychological orientation. In the child, he is anticipating a normal development to a well-balanced maturity.

Social and personal conditions of human life are far different today than they were in the Middle Ages. Most obvious is the difficulty of achieving a normal personality in a social environment which is so removed from natural principles and so corruptive to the practice of faith. The force of faith has been diminished by the spirit of compromise and the ascendency of emotional attitudes over reasoned convictions, conditions which characterize our time. The pervasive Christian atmosphere of the Age of Faith has been dissipated by the contrary values of secular humanism which are paramount in contemporary society. Opposed to the supernatural values of poverty, virginity and obedience in religious life, are the modern tendencies towards material acquisitions, sexual promiscuity, and the revolt against authority. This is the Age of Selfishness.

Artificiality of custom and pettiness of concern cramp the natural generosity of youth and pervert the ideals and goals which motivate them. The sense of sin is as much lost as is the incentive to heroic virtue. The pursuit of false values and the consequent disorder of life result in tensions and frustrations. To achieve a normal personality and mature development of faith, therefore, is not the ordinary achievement which could have been expected in past periods of the Christian era. Our modern manner of life has disturbed, and often disordered, the fragile structure of the human personality.

Until very recently the only testing of candidates for religious life was for physical fitness. Today the concept of fitness, or suitability, has widened and deepened to encompass the total personality and has caused it to be subjected to exploration and probing.

Many religious institutes now require psychological testing of candidates, using either standard psychodiagnostic tests, such as the Minnesota Multiphasic Personality Inventory, or special tests prepared by associated experts and applied to the particular needs of a community. Judgment and prognosis must still be made to determine the applicant's stability and adaptability to the drastic changes of perspective and practical living which distinguish the cloister from the world outside.

The qualifications of suitability are, therefore, very extensive and include physical, psychical and moral aptitudes. Furthermore, aptitudes applicable to the particular institute or community should be taken into consideration. A candidate may be suited for one particular kind of religious observance and activity but not for another. The requirements of a contemplative community, for example, will differ from those of an institute engaged in apostolic activity. In general, the older orders and societies have their own distinct spirit and form of religious discipline which attract particular types to their community.

Most writers on this subject of suitability are agreed that the more measurable physical qualities required are easily ascertained by standard medical tests. The relative severity of physical requirements may vary with the demands of particular institutes, for example those engaged in mission activity, but all look for a normal disposition of health. This means a freedom from any chronic infirmities which would impede the religious from fulfilling his religious obligations and make him more of a burden than an asset to the community. One who could not live in the religious state without permanent dispensations from the requirement of a rule is certainly not fit for this state of life.

Two French doctors, Renè Biot and Pierre Galimard, have done a comprehensive *Medical Guide to Vocations* (Newman Press, 1955) to aid directors of seminaries and convents in detecting certain physical and psychological signs of unsuitability in the religious aspirant. A detailed account of physical disabilities is given in this work, along with a description of mental and moral defects from a medical point of view. This study should prove a valuable reference and should be consulted directly. I will quote only their summary conclusion on mental and moral impediments:

Examining the problem from the mental and moral points of view, we would list the following definite counter-indications: recognized mental aberration in the individual; mental weakness; definite epilepsy recurring despite regular treatment or having left an epileptoid tendency; serious alcoholic heredity; pronounced psychiatric heredity; definite paranoiac constitution; typical cyclothymic constitution; symptoms of schizoidism; moral perversions in the strict sense; perversions of the sexual instinct; homosexuality in overt or covert forms; inveterate habits of masturbation. (p. 135.)

I would like to make two other references before going into the problems of emotional and moral disorder in detail. For a discussion of emotional disorders which determine vocational unfitness I have used the text of a talk entitled "Types Suited or Unsuited for Religious Vocation," given at the Eighth Annual Vocation Institute (1954) at Notre Dame by Father Charles J. D. Corcoran, O.P. For the conclusions pertinent to moral fitness I have consulted the class notes of Father Paul Philippe, O.P., from a lecture given in 1954 at The Spiritual Institute, held at The Dominican House of Studies, River Forest, Illinois.

Man's emotional makeup is a mixture of contrary forces: love and hate, courage and fear, joy and sadness, hope and despair, etc. Sound emotional health, the aim of mental hygiene, consists in a proper balance of these emotions. Struggling against concupiscence, an effect of original sin, man strives to order the fluctuations of antagonistic emotions and organic resonances by achieving a supremacy of the will over these dynamic forces. This balance is achieved normally with the maturity of reason and with the divine assistance of grace motivating the mind and moving the will.

Emotional disorders occur when the mature person fails to achieve the supremacy of will over his affective life. Physiological changes, underlying all emotion and more properly called temperament, are at the basis of this disorder. This is why some forms of physiotherapy, such as shock treatment and drugs, can help to alleviate the tensions of a neurotic condition.

In temperament there are two principal elements: fluctuation and equilibrium. The sound personality has just enough malleability and the right amount of stability. The choleric type will be prone to an occasional outburst of anger, but if this quickly passes and control is readily regained there is no marked disorder in the personality. On the other hand, the person who harbors resentments and holds grudges exhibits an abnormal and dangerous affective rigidity. St. Augustine, in his Rule, says that such a type is unsuited for religious life:

One who is quick to anger, but prompt in asking pardon of the one whom he has offended, is better off than one who is slower to anger and slower to seek pardon for his offense. Moreover, one who never begs pardon of anyone, or who does it only begrudgingly, has no business in religious life, even if the superiors do not dismiss him.

"A religious vocation," says Father Corcoran, "may be hampered or entirely ruled out by excess or defect in either aspect of temperament. Flexibility and suppleness of personality are required for a sound state; so is firmness and stability. A person can be so malleable he may take to the mold of religious life initially, and when assaulted by temptations beyond the cloister be equally flexible in shedding the mold for other patterns of behavior."

Montalembert, in the introduction to his *Monks of the West*, gives three classic traits which indicate a healthy religious personality: simplicity, benignity, and a sense of humor.

Simplicity is a necessary quality of religious who are called to be of one mind and heart in taking on, as it were, the personality of Jesus Christ. Affectation, egotism, eccentricity are unhealthy signs of selfishness which signal an imbalance of personality. Benignity is expressed in kindness and patience, in supporting, according to St. Paul's injunction, one another's burdens with true charity and generosity of spirit. Humor is based on man's reasoned perception of incongruities. A lack of a sense of humor indicates a defect of the practical reason, symptomatic of nearly every form of derangement. Because of the religious man's recognition, naturally speaking, of the implicit incongruity of man's ascent to God, he must learn to laugh at his own nothingness before the august presence of God—He who is, while we are who are not.* A sense of humor combats the thousand petty afflictions of a confined community life in the religious state.

Father Philippe, before treating the question of moral fitness, considers the more common mental and emotional disturbances. Without question, he considers paranoid or schizoid tendencies as grave impediments to religious life. The paranoid would falsely judge that other members of the community, especially superiors, are "against him." The schizoid would isolate himself from a community by singular and queer behavior.

Among those suffering from nervous disorders, the principal types are the emotive, the neurasthenic

---

* Our Lord said to St. Catherine of Siena, and various other saintly religious, "I am He who is; you are she who is not." This means that God is the only Being who exists in and of Himself. All other beings, including man, exist contingent upon God's ongoing sustaining power. —*Publisher*, 2005.

or psychasthenic, and the hysterical. Emotive people have an exaggerated emotional reaction, out of proportion to the stimuli affecting them. Such persons can be trained and corrected and may be suitable for religious life provided that their hyperemotion is not too strong. Neurasthenics and psychasthenics are restless, anxious, obsessed types of personality.

The neurasthenic is usually a hypochondriac and generally is irritable and moody. The psychasthenic suffers morally, usually obsessed by scruples over his present condition or worry over past moral offenses, real or imagined. The neurasthenic and the psychasthenic are risks in the religious state; the demands of religious life may either destroy or develop their imbalance. There should be evidence of progress in overcoming these conditions before they are admitted to religious life. The truly hysterical, who feign charismatic gifts to gain attention, should never be admitted to the religious state. To judge the genuine mystic from the hysterical person is often difficult and requires the careful observation of a trained theologian.

One is morally suitable for admission into religious life who manifests both natural and religious virtues to a sufficient degree and has a sincere desire to perfect himself in this state of life by using the means provided. The indispensable natural virtues required, according to Father Philippe, are: a right conscience, a profoundly honest character, sincerity and sociability. The required religious virtues are: true piety, docility for direction, a spirit of penance to accept the renunciations required, the practice of chastity, and true devotion to a way of life dedicated to the service of neighbor for the love of God.

The moral requirement with regard to chastity deserves special consideration, both because of the natural weakness involved and because of the current laxity in sexual morality which makes the practice of chastity so much more difficult today.

According to most moral theologians, certain types of people affected by lapses in sexual morality should be absolutely excluded from the religious state. These are: (1) Hypersexual persons, prone by nature to an abnormal obsession with sexual matters and usually habituated to sexual indulgence in a compulsory manner. (2) Persons who have lived a degrading and infamous life, cohabiting with others for sexual purposes. Such who are in a true state of repentance may try the cloistered contemplative life but never an institute engaged in active apostolic works. (3) Persons who while considering the religious life seduce another, indicating an overpowering sexual impulse like the hypersexual. Other criteria verified, they may possibly enter a contemplative institute but not an active one. (4) Persons who, without being hypersexual, fall into solitary sin occasionally (every month or two), without taking the necessary means to correct this condition and irrevocably break the habit. The disposition of such a person is important in determining the possibility of acceptance. Lack of applying ordinary means of overcoming the habit and consequent moods of discouragement indicate the candidate should be rejected.

Ordinarily the judgment on moral suitability must be made by the confessor, who can reach the aspirant in the internal forum and become better acquainted with the disposition and attitude of the penitent. Sometimes a manifestation of conscience may be made to a vocational director, but this should not be demanded and when it is offered must be treated with great delicacy and prudence. It would be better for the director to advise the aspirant to acquire a regular confessor and follow the latter's judgment and counsel. The institute will have an opportunity to test and observe the candidate in the intimate life of the religious community.

And so there are reservations which restrict the general invitation to the practice of the evangelical counsels in the religious state. These are based primarily on the suitability of the subject to undertake the burdens of religious life. The supposition is in favor of a right intention and personal fitness; but the fact may be otherwise, especially in these times when personality disorders are, unfortunately, rather common.

But what of those who seem suitable, pass the periods of trial, adjust to the regular life of the religious—and then leave: what of their vocation?"

CHAPTER IX

The "Lost Vocation"

THERE are many who enter religious life and then leave it. Those who leave during the trial periods— the postulancy or novitiate—and these are the majority, usually return to the ranks of the laity because of "lack of vocation." Those who make profession of vows and live the regular religious life for some time, and then leave at the expiration of their vows or seek dispensation from them, speak of a "loss of vocation." Are these accurate expressions? Can one really be lacking a religious vocation? Can one actually lose it?

Again we have to go back to that mysterious "it"— the sense of vocation.

Antecedently, or abstractly, God generally invites all to the practice of the evangelical counsels in the religious state. Consequently, or concretely, he prepares and moves some to respond to this invitation and become religious. He prepares those who are chosen to serve Him in this state of life by providing them with a certain suitability, by nature and by grace, and assists them in wanting to live such a life.

God acts upon us and aids us, on both natural and supernatural levels of operation, but He does not force us and leaves the free will inviolate. He very literally cooperates with us, operatively in our good actions and permissively in our bad actions.

The person, therefore, who departs from religious life after trying it, either lacked a fitness for the life in the first place, or did not cooperate with the means of grace, necessary for perseverance, which God provides through this state of life. I am excluding from consideration those who may incur some prohibitive impediment, such as poor health or family needs, which makes their departure necessary and proper, especially in the early stages of religious life. Religious in perpetual vows would not be required to leave under these or any other circumstances.

Strictly speaking, one cannot lack or lose a vocation, if we see the meaning of vocation in the divine decrees which God efficaciously executes. What we do does not change the will of God but fulfills it. After the fact we can very well say that "such is God's will." But we must avoid an implication of divine determinism, of fatalism. We are inviolably free in all our choices. We could choose other than we do. Perhaps this particular person could have persevered in the religious state if he had wanted to. By "wanting" I mean an efficacious willing; and this involves a use of ordinary means, not a "wishing" to accomplish some end while neglecting the necessary means to attain it.

This problem is much easier to solve in regard to religious life than it is in the case of sacerdotal vocation. For, as we have pointed out, the religious state does not require extraordinary graces or the special call which brings a candidate to the priesthood. In ordinary circumstances the normal Christian, with the right intention and a will docile to grace and direction, can succeed in the practice of the evangelical counsels.

Why does the religious novice leave an institute after a relatively short period of trial? There are many possible reasons: (1) He doesn't give the life a fair trial and is quickly overcome by accidental defects, his own or those of other members of the community. This is most common among aspirants who leave after a few weeks or months. (2) He suffers from some canonical defect—ill health, family need, etc. (3) He has entered an institute unsuitable for him: active instead of contemplative, or characterized by a manner of life or form of apostolic work for which he is unfitted. (4) From the beginning he himself was unsuited to religious life—

physically, mentally, emotionally or morally. (5) He lacked a right intention and was drawn to such a life by romantic, sensible, accidental attractions. This is especially verified in the immature who impulsively apply to apostolic schools for the wrong reasons. (6) He fails to cooperate with the graces of his state and the direction of his superiors.

Those who leave religious life after spending many years in the cloister pose a more formidable problem. Certainly some of the solutions listed above would not apply to the professed religious who has achieved at least apparent success in living in the religious state for a considerable period of time. The failure to cooperate with grace, through neglect of the means of religious life, is a decline and retrogression, however, which can occur at any point of time during one's religious life. There is no such thing as "coasting" in this or any other state of life. Such a decline, moreover, is gradual, not sudden, and ordinarily detectable by vigilant superiors.

St. Thomas treats the so-called "lost vocation" with customary bluntness and brevity. God's invitation, he says, is not lost in the sense of its being withdrawn. God's counsel, in itself, is unchangeable; but not so man's will. God's grace is never wanting; man's generosity often is. Says St. Thomas: "The will of God is unchangeable. On this point we must consider that to change the will is one thing; to will that certain things should be changed is another."[76]

Sometimes, he points out, leaving the religious state is expedient. He mentions that such departures "for a reasonable cause," namely sickness or weakness, or something of this kind "indicate a lack of subjective suitability."[77] And for such reasons, he says, he who leaves does not give bad example or cause scandal, unless it be passive and unreasonable scandal. Such an attitude on the part of observers is a common item of experience.

As for others who leave simply because, as they say, they "didn't have a vocation," St. Thomas considers both the divine and human, the objective and subjective, sides of this situation.

Those who leave under these circumstances, says the Angelic Doctor "change their resolve" (*propter hoc quod homo mutat propositum.*) Then he goes on to say that to some "the gift of persevering is not given"[78] (*quibus in ea perseverandi donum non datur.*)

In context, however, the indication is that this gift of perseverance is not extraordinary. When man fails to do his part (by not cooperating with sufficient grace), God refuses the necessary efficacious grace which ordinarily would be given. Excepting unusual circumstances, therefore, a "lost" vocation is caused directly by the human will failing to cooperate and indirectly by the withholding of the divine gift. This withholding of the gift of perseverance, as a matter of fact, is not even an indirect cause because God is not obliged to give the gift of His grace.

Surely God does give this gift of the grace of perseverance to those who do not change their resolve, their firm determination, their holy confidence, and who dispose themselves by generously fulfilling the obligations of their state of life. St. Thomas even says: "It is better to enter religion with the purpose of making a trial than not to enter it at all, because by so doing one disposes oneself to remain always."[79]

On this question of perseverance the application of these principles to particular cases is not easy. Again we encounter the complex constitution of each individual personality. Why *this* person leaves religious life, after many years in it, is a necessary mystery shared by that person and God. Ultimately only God knows because we cannot fully comprehend the mixture of motivations that prompt our own behavior. The best we can do is to analyze particular cases, either by observation or by examining the subject's own self-analysis. The experience of spiritual directors and confessors of religious institutes would provide abundant material for study and comparative analysis. But such material must remain confidential and unpublished.

There are some ex-religious, however, who have provided us with published reports of their own experiences in living and leaving the religious state. By manifesting their conscience, at least in part and as they see it, and offering this display of "religious experience" to the public with a written record we can examine critically a few cases of the "lost vocation."

The first popular exposé of "how I lost my vocation" was the work of Monica Baldwin and had the catchy title, *I Leap Over the Wall* (Rinehart & Co., N. Y., 1950.) In her introduction, Miss Baldwin, after spending twenty-eight years in a convent, simply said: "I describe the religious vocation from the point of view of one who had no such vocation." Such a statement seems to contradict just about everything we have said in this book. A careful study, however, of her approach and attitude towards vocation, and her impressions and expressions of religious life, cause the reader to wonder if she ever really had any idea of what a religious vocation is.

On page eight of her reflections she speaks of two classes of women who become nuns:

The first and smaller class consists of those who are naturally devout. Marriage does not particularly attract them. They like saying their prayers (as opposed, perhaps, to praying!); they love a quiet, well-ordered existence, with heaven as its goal. They do not make the best nuns, but they certainly lead good lives and quite often arrive at a surprising degree of holiness.

No one is "naturally devout" in respect to supernatural faith. Some, by natural constitution, find quiet, prayer and meditation more easy to acquire as habitual attitudes. This is not true devotion, which is an interior act of the supernatural virtue of religion and may be present as often in a naturally restless personality as it is in a naturally relaxed one.

If girls become nuns because "marriage does not particularly attract them" they are poor candidates for a state of life which requires a normal personality. If they do so because they naturally like "a quiet well-ordered existence" and a round of prayers, they lack a right intention. Either they, or Miss Baldwin confuse natural dispositions with a supernatural state. Grace works on nature, not nature on grace.

Back to Miss Baldwin's second class of religious,

or the ones she knew, or, at least, her interpretation of those she knew:

The second class is the larger and the more interesting. It consists of the people who enter convents less because they themselves choose to do so than because they are chosen by God. These are the real "vocations." Some spiritual adventure has happened to them: some vital encounter has taken place between their soul and God. They know, beyond all possibility of doubt, that God is not just some vague, remote, spiritual ideal, but a living Person. They therefore become possessed by a kind of burning hunger and thirst for God, which only he himself can satisfy.

Miss Baldwin's second class of vocations is an extraordinary one, involving unusual mystical experiences. In proposing these as "the real vocations," she promotes the unnecessary mystery of the something-special school of thought. Granting an unusual "encounter" or experience prompting some to enter religious life, such cases are few and far between and even these pose a problem of whether such incidents are genuinely from God or merely self-induced under propitious circumstances.

Her account of a period of spiritual desolation (pp. 219 ff.) and her reaction to the orthodox explanation and counsel given to her, leaves the reader wondering again about Miss Baldwin's grasp of things theological and supernatural. The same impression is received from reading her expression of her problem with the virtue of humility (pp. 273 ff.). She also seems to expect mysticism to precede asceticism (p. 290.)

At the end of her book (pp. 298 ff.), Miss Baldwin finally answers the obviously persistent question in the mind of the reader. She says: "You would be surprised at the number of people who have asked me why it was that I left the convent." We would not be surprised at all, considering the fact that on writing this sentence she had been in the convent half of her life, from World War I to World War II.

In italics she gives the long-awaited answer (p. 299): "*Should you ever feel attracted to the idea of entering a convent, be sure and test yourself till you know for certain whether your chief motive for so doing is a sincere conviction that it is the Will of God for you. If you enter merely because you feel an attraction for the life, you may expect rocks ahead.*"

Her failure, she said, was to neglect to do that and she went on to explain that her entering the convent seemed to be self-willed and self-propelled. The implication here, and from the other references I have made, is that Miss Baldwin was herself the type that naturally likes a quiet, prayerful, well-ordered life.

In other words, the motivation seemed altogether natural and apparently never changed. It took 28 years to reach a natural saturation point. Others undoubtedly have entered the religious state with the same foundation, but few, I am sure, could have endured it as long as Miss Baldwin did. She was a noble soul who confused the good life with the better life, the natural with the supernatural, and never fully recognized the essence of religious vocation.

A tragic account of a departure from faith, as well as from religious life and sacerdotal status, was given by John (Fr. Ildefonso) Tettemer in his book, *I Was A Monk* (Alfred A. Knopf, N. Y., 1951.) He was a Passionist who held high and responsible positions in his Order and Church, and then set aside all of his religious obligations under the stress of intellectual difficulties which destroyed his belief in the supernatural.

This is a curious story which leaves the reader with a sense of incompletion and dissatisfaction. One has the impression that it is a three-part story with the middle part left out. The metamorphosis from good religious to non-religious is too sudden; for the corruption of the habit of faith is necessarily gradual and manifested long before the final dissolution.

Whatever happened to Fr. Ildefonso which is not disclosed is inscrutable, but we can at least conjecture some opinions from what is given in the narrative. In his approach to religious life he shows a certain yet undefinable naivete, an unmistakable immaturity despite the fact that he was not a youngster when he entered. There is, for example, an expression of romanticism in his view of the Carthusian life, which he first considered:

The monks rarely met each other except to gather in the choir of the church to sing the Divine Office at the appointed hours. The nearest my imagination could come to a heaven on earth was the poetic picture of cowled monks emerging silently from their little houses, wending their grave way—at nighttime with lanterns—along the colonnaded cloister walk to the choir. (p. 28)

Discovering that there were no Carthusian foundations in the U. S. at that time, he sought a strict order which still adhered to a pristine vigor of discipline and survived the modern tendency to any relaxation of its rule or compromise with its original ideals. He said:

My ardor was such that I was determined to join no order into which any spirit of the world had begun to creep. I could not bear the idea of half measures in service and love of God. My renunciation of the world would be complete, my dedication in the monastery to God absolute. The books I searched convinced me that the Passionists adhered strictly to this ideal. I would apply to them for admission to be a lay brother. (p. 29)

His own description of his early religious training in the order displays an exaggerated concern over the petty and trivial details of religious practice and a lack of proper emphasis on principles of the spiritual life and its development. His recollections and reflections do not show evidence of the extraordinary talent and character which his superiors undoubtedly judged to be in him. He was selected to be one of the first American students to study at the Order's International College in Rome. By dispensation, he was ordained early after only two years of theology. Upon completing the required studies and in spite of his protestations of insufficiency, he was appointed spiritual director and professor of classics in the province's preparatory seminary. After only four years in this position he was appointed director of the International College in Rome!

His duties multiplied as director, professor, consultor at the Vatican, confessor, preacher—until at last he admitted some neglect of his own spiritual life. He said:

The work of being a chaplain to the nuns and to the hospital cut rather deeply into my time, depriving me of much of the seclusion that had hitherto constituted my monastic life. This fact, and my absorption in the deeper studies required by the teaching of St. Thomas, often found my little *bugia* burning late into the night, and the consequent loss of time for mental prayer and other primary monastic duties was of some concern to me. And still there was no consciousness of any dread disease lurking in my soul. (p. 196)

Back in America, as a teacher, and later, as superior of a new monastery, he indicated a sense of interior loss:

Some sort of weakening must have been occasioned in my spiritual life by the multiplicity of my occupations, and the consequent shortening of my nourishing hours of prayer. (p. 203)

After only 12 years of apostolic work in his order, and at the age of 38, he was appointed Consultor General of the Order, the second highest office possible to him. This meteoric rise in his order is astounding. Undoubtedly such sudden and heavy pressures on a priest so young and inexperienced contributed to the collapse that soon followed.

The transition from a brilliant light in his order to the darkness of disbelief and rejection of religious obligations is abrupt, too abrupt, in the narration. Suddenly there is a deep metaphysical problem over monism, a confusion over the key philosophical concept of analogy, an awareness of the mystery of being which induces a complete skepticism. All this evolves and erupts, we are told, and much of it elaborated during a period of convalescence in Switzerland. A breakdown is indicated but never fully described. It just happens, supposedly.

With this cessation of activity and divorce from the demands of religious life comes a release into a subjective "other world," a real union with eternal being that surpasses the clinging to the shadows of changing being in time. This is the poetic attempt to reach an esoteric, ego-centric state. What had young John Tettemer sought in the first place? Was it the religious state, objectively constituted with approved means for attaining a real perfection in charity? Or was it his own subjective version of a kind of personal nirvana?

He provides this key to recognizing a faulty understanding and therefore a wrong intention. As he described it:

Contrary to boyhood dreams, my monastic life had become a life of exceptional activity, predominantly mental, to be sure, but nevertheless of a pattern to link me to a world of change, impeding the realization in my consciousness of that real and eternal world which I saw as my true home. In my hours of prayer I glimpsed that world sufficiently to attest to its beautiful reality, but it seemed always just out of my reach. I must devote myself to the duties of the nearer, active world; always it was my duty to come back to studying men's philosophies and other knowledge, to lecture to students, to preach sermons, hear confessions, and in many practical ways take part in the world that for me fell short of reality. Now an all but full stop had been put for me to habitual activity. In itself inactivity became for me a chrysalis state. (p. 237)

John Tettemer did not seek a Christian ideal at all, because even Contemplation at times must give way to necessary works of charity. His spiritual ideals are more akin to quietism and to Indian mysticism.

The last prominent literary record of a "lost vocation" was a fictional account of a true story, which became a best-seller and a popular movie. Nearly every one has had an opinion of *The Nun's Story* (Atlantic, Little, Brown & Co., Boston, Toronto, 1956.) We will offer another from a vocational point of view.

By profession of religious vows a person makes a total dedication of self, a holocaust, the most complete sacrifice that man can make to God. The essence of this sacrifice is the vow of obedience by which one offers the gift of his own will, the very core of self. This is the most perfect external act of religion, but without effect in religious life if it does not express the internal reality it professes.

Sister Luke, in *The Nun's Story*, never achieves this total dedication. There is always a lurking condition. Her gift is contingent upon what she wants, and is therefore a contradiction never satisfactorily resolved. She herself is conscious of constantly bargaining with God. The root of the conflict is exposed many times throughout the story. Towards the end she sums up her own problem in her conversations with the chaplain and with Mother Superior. To the chaplain who warns her that the spiritual struggle is more difficult in the world, she replies:

I agree, she said. But would it not be a hypocrisy to remain in the convent only through fear of the world? It must be voluntary, through love of God alone and without any grumbling and inner murmuring, Father. Otherwise, it has no merit in His eyes. My staying has no merit. He knows why I remain . . . (p. 310)

Sister Luke does recognize that true devotion is an act of the will, that obedience is a habit of the will and must be given without reservation or condition. This is the essence of religious life and its absence indicates the lack of a true religious resolve.

In continuing her conversation she makes this point more explicitly:

> I believe, Father, . . . that even the smallest gesture of charity made in the world, with joy, would be ten times more pleasing to God than all the work I do here under a Holy Rule I only pretend to obey.

In her last conference with Mother Superior she again states her position clearly:

> In the beginning, . . . each struggle seemed different from the preceding. No two ever seemed for the same cause, until they began to repeat and then I saw they all had the same core. Obedience, Reverend Mother. Obedience without question, obedience without inner murmuring, obedience blind, instantaneous, perfect in its acceptance as Christ practiced it . . . as I can no longer do. My conscience asks questions, Reverend Mother. When the bell calls to chapel and I have to sacrifice what might be the psychological moment in a spiritual talk with a patient, my conscience asks which has priority—it or the Holy Rule. In my mind, I have never been able to make this clear. . . . I believe that most of my failure stems from this conflict. (p. 315)

One might question her concept of obedience, the insistence on its being "blind" and "perfect" and, implicitly, contrary at times to true prudence of action. The fact remains that the offering of self-will, which is at the center of the oblation of the religious state, is not there. Hence there is no real *propositum religionis* in this response to the invitation to the practice of the evangelical counsels.

The application of principles to these recorded accounts of "lost vocations" helps to clarify the confusion caused by those who try and then leave the religious state. The response to Christ's invitation must be that of a normal personality possessing a right intention and making use of the efficacious means of the grace of perseverance.

CHAPTER X

Conclusions and Applications

THE most obvious conclusion we have reached is that there is a lot of unnecessary mystery surrounding—perhaps I should say *obscuring*—the idea of religious vocation. The experiential fact is that most religious candidates, and not a few of their counsellors, are rather hazy about just what they are looking for when they set out in search of "a vocation." Such acknowledged confusion is bound to have damaging effects on the development of religious life.

In an earlier chapter I quoted a contemporary author on the religious state as claiming that the influx of postulants to religious life has remained constant despite changing values in the social scene.* In general, this is a correct observation. But specifically, within our own time and place, religious vocations have declined. Perseverance is an even more striking problem for all institutes. The demand made on active congregations, especially those which supply teachers and nurses, far exceeds the available supply. No doubt the radical change of values in our society

---

* See the footnote on p. 25. Shortly after this book was published in 1961, there occurred a dramatic decline in religious vocations.
—*Publisher*, 2005.

is largely responsible. But in a scientific age of well-defined terms perhaps our cloudy understanding of the meaning of religious vocation is a considerable factor contributing to the lack of interest and incentive among our youth. The response to religious vocational appeal is not what it should be. In the decade between 1950 and 1960 the increase of Catholics in the U.S. was 38%; the parallel increase of religious vocations in that period was only 18%.

The point is that we are not doing as well as we should. Proportionate to our Catholic population, we Americans are not filling our expected quota of professed religious. St. John Bosco, who could speak with authority on the subject of youth and religion, once said that he believed one out of every four Catholic boys had the "seed" of religious vocation! Much of that seed, obviously, never fructifies. The reasons, of course, are many. The causes influencing the behavior of any individual are many and complicated, and so much more multiplied when we are considering whole social groups.

My only, and indisputable, negative conclusion is that vocational ignorance is at least partly responsible for this critical situation. And this ignorance has been encrusted with layers of unnecessary mystery. It is easy, and practically convenient, to speak mysteriously about those things of which we are ignorant, or at least unspecific and therefore unsure.

Much of the popular propaganda on the subject of religious vocation veers towards one or the other of two erroneous extremes. On the one hand there is the almost exclusive concern with the objective counsel, minimizing, at times even excluding, the necessary subjective disposition which must involve divine preordination and premotion. On the other hand, the attraction theory, which has been so thoroughly discredited, continues to exert an even more virulent influence on contemporary vocational discussion and expression. This dangerous emphasis on subjective, even perceptible inspiration perdures in vocational literature.

The essential and necessary mystery of vocation is that God does preordain and premove a subject to particular patterns of activity which affect his ultimate end. But here we encounter the unfathomable mysteries of the divine operation in us: God's universal causality, premotion and predestination. Divine causality, however, in no way violates human freedom. Nor is the divine will, as one author has claimed, "dependent or consequent upon man's choice." God moves the free will of intelligent creatures according to their nature—freely—and that's that.

We cannot, and therefore should not, probe this

divine action in us in order to see its course directly. We do not make such an attempt prior to other choices; why should we make such an impossible demand with regard to the choice of the religious state of life?

Religious vocation is a matter of divine ordination, the manifestation of God's will with regard to our state of life. We know God's will only through its effects. Of these effects, counsel actively invites all Christians, seeking the best possible means to attain perfection, to the literal and absolute practice of poverty, virginity and obedience in the religious state; divine operation, on both natural and supernatural levels, exerts a necessary influence on the subject who freely and deliberately responds to this divine invitation. This is the essence of religious vocation.

The Thomistic position stands in the middle way of truth, avoiding the opposite extremes of error. We hold to a general objective invitation to the religious state through revealed counsel, and, at the same time, to God's free choice and necessary causality in influencing some to respond to this counsel. Father Maggiolo (in a work cited, p. 283) succinctly sums up the doctrinal position of St. Thomas: "Religious vocation is not an exceptional grace reserved to a privileged few but . . . an invitation extended by

Jesus Christ to all without distinction." Counsel, objectively, is static and sterile of itself, and so the divine operation in the subject is required; for vocation "has efficacy only by an internal impulse of the Holy Ghost that causes to rise in the heart an appreciation of and desire for the religious life."

Theologically, with technical bluntness, we can say that God by His antecedent will (an abstract consideration) invites all to the religious state; but by His consequent will (concretely), in conjunction with but not dependent upon the human will, causes some to respond to this invitation.

In the external forum, exercising its juridical power, the Church imposes certain requirements in a subject responding to this invitation, thus establishing fulfillment of what is called ecclesiastical vocation. The right intention, most important of these requirements in an otherwise fit subject, involves the act of response which St. Thomas simply calls *propositum religionis*. This is an act of the rational will, following and deliberating upon true knowledge, and has no necessary connection with emotional response except by accidental natural redundance.

In any supernatural action, a good human act pertains to infused virtue. In the response to religious vocation, which requires the permanency of habit, this acceptance of the divine invitation is made by an act of devotion proceeding from the virtue of religion. And since this action is one of total conse-creation, demanding supreme generosity, it is intensified by the virtue of magnanimity.

As a positive conclusion, therefore, a complete descriptive definition, including all of these essential elements, can be proposed:

Religious vocation is a divine invitation, extended to all by Jesus Christ, to the practice of the evangelical counsels in the religious state, to which a capable subject, under the impetus of grace, responds through generous devotion.

In recent times religious institutes have followed the popular trend toward public relations and have propagandized the advantages of religious life in order to obtain candidates—some even go so far as to use the word "recruits." The intention, and to some extent the methods employed, are laudable; but the expressed results are often deplorable. The essence of the religious state is sometimes lost in a cluttering promotion of accidental facets of the life proposed. The effort to assure potential candidates that religious men are "regular guys" and religious women are up-to-date "career girls" is so overdone one gets the impression that religious institutes are social clubs with natural purposes for people who have nowhere else to go and nothing else to do. The appeal should be to supernatural motives, to happiness through holiness, an achievement possible only through the unhindered flow of grace on a subject prepared to make a total sacrifice, a perfect oblation of self.

Even in more scholarly presentations of the subject, the religious state is seldom seen in the context of theology, in the whole economy of salvation. There is always an unmistakable emphasis on exclusiveness, on something "special" and "extra." Little wonder that the average generous soul cringes in abject retreat, before such august presumptions. As a result, religious institutes often attract the imprudent and the truly "special" fringe characters who are easily drawn to the esoteric. If we are not getting more sound, rounded, wholesome types as candidates but more odd, narrow, unbalanced postulants, then obviously our approach to the Christian faithful is somehow distorted and misleading. The truth shall make us free. Theological truth, acquired and shared, can free us from our vocational mistakes and their unfortunate consequences.

St. Thomas, as we have shown, always approached the invitation to the religious state objectively, emphasizing the explicit counsel of Christ to all of His followers. The contemporary approach, on the other hand, is subjective, emphasizing the internal development of response. Properly vocation should refer to the external *luctio,* the expression of counsel revealed by Jesus Christ, rather than to its passive termination in the response of the subject. This divine operation of interior influence in the subject is the motion of reaction in response. Subjective vocation is analagous, referring the formal concept to what is effected terminatively.

The writer or speaker discussing religious life, therefore, should make his appeal general and objective. His approach should not be: "Is God calling you—look into your heart of hearts, etc." Rather, the approach should be the Christlike challenge to all, appealing to personal courage and generosity to effect a response: "God *is* calling you, daring you to follow Him. Are you generous enough, etc.?" To insure a true response, founded upon more than emotional reaction, the religious state, the object of their consideration, should be presented as it really is. Our purpose should be to inform the intellect, illumined by faith, so that a true object is presented to the rational will, eliciting a deliberate act of virtue.

Then there is the matter of terminology. Do we even have to use the word "vocation"? In ecclesiastical usage, this word more directly and properly applies to the divine selection of candidates to the priesthood. Here the terminative and effective use of *vocatio* is justified. For there is no directly revealed call to certain individuals to the priesthood, except in extraordinary cases like that of St. Paul. Active vocation must always remain a divine mystery; and there is no general objective norm effected by the divine will as there is in the case of counsel to the religious state. Hence it is *only* by terminative effects of divine gifts of nature and of grace that subjective vocation to the priesthood can be discerned. Therefore it is more proper to speak of one "having a vocation," in a selective sense, with reference to the priesthood than to the religious state.

Better still, conforming with strict ecclesiastical terminology, we should say that one *shows signs* of a divine vocation to the priesthood. Such signs are much more specific and definitive in sacerdotal vocation than they are in the general requirements of suitability and right intention demanded in candidates to the religious state.

The indiscriminate use of the word "vocation" to apply both to the priesthood and to the religious state is unwise; for this tends to identify the formalities expressed. This confusion has already occurred in the popular mind. Significantly, Canon Law em-

ploys the word "vocation" in speaking of the priesthood, but not in reference to the religious state.
Pastors are admonished to foster in youths the seed
of divine vocation to the priesthood. (Canon 1353.)
There is no such reference to a "seed of vocation" to
the religious state, precisely because this seed is
identical with grace, the seed of glory, and resides
in all the souls of the just.

While St. Thomas does use the terms *vocatio* and
locutio, he also, just as often, prefers the word
invitatio.[80] The word "invitation" is also used by the
Fathers of the Church. A contemporary Thomist,
Father Walter Farrell, O.P., has succinctly defined
religious vocation as "an invitation to serve in the
divine household." Our English word "vocation,"
especially as it is used among Catholics, is associated
with the priesthood and implies a sense of imperious
command or injunction; whereas "invitation" gives
the better sense of an absence of necessity or obligation in the corresponding acceptance. Some other
words, such as "challenge" and "dare," add a notion
of testing courage to face adventurous hardship, and
these surely apply to the motion towards religious
life. It is my opinion that St. Thomas, if he were
among us today, would avoid using the word "vocation" in a popular approach to religious life be-

cause of its contemporary connotation of "special" and "obligatory."

The vantage point changes when we consider the particular task of the confessor and spiritual director. When it comes to guiding the individual soul, a director must apply the general invitation of the counsels to subjective suitability and rightness of intention in the particular person who responds.

The vocational director should be fair in setting the norms of suitability. Psychological soundness in the candidate poses a problem of balanced judgment in the director. We cannot take the attitude that everyone is odd except ourselves. To a degree, everyone *is* odd, including ourselves, because literally we are all peculiarly individual. There is no common denominator of personality, and, in this sense, no such thing as normalcy. In judging others, people too often set themselves up as the desirable norm and find everyone else "strange."

There are general objective norms of a balanced personality, with which the director should familiarize himself. At least there are negative signs of an absence of serious disorders. Certain neurotic tendencies, as we have pointed out, may be absorbed in and even corrected by community life. Others will be too disturbing to the community and threaten the commonweal. The vocational director has to be a psychologist of sorts as well as a theologian to assure the correctness of the judgments he must make. Sufficient personal contact with the candidate should make his judgment firm enough to decide whether to try him in a novitiate. By demanding periods of trial under various superiors and directors, the Church wisely and cautiously avoids the irrevocable decision of any single constituted authority.

The director also must be wary of the full implication of "a right intention." Remember that the *propositum religionis* is a deliberate act of will, motivated by true knowledge. An efficacious act of the will includes the intention of using means necessary to achieve the desired end. Otherwise a person possesses only a velleity, an inefficacious *wishing* rather than an efficacious *willing*.

Therefore it is not enough to hear a candidate express a desire to "save my own soul and help save the souls of others." This is the normal and necessary desire of every devout Christian. The point is does *this* Christian intend to attain this purpose through *these particular means* of religious life? Furthermore, he must be ready to use these means as they are proposed by the institute and confirmed by the Church, not as they are practiced by particular religious or as he himself would prefer them to be.

This is an important point. For there are many good Christians who are naturally bent to "go it alone" in the way of perfection and cannot, or will not, conform to any fixed patterns of spiritual progress. They may be orthodox in the practice of their faith but yet retain a firm grip on self-reliance and self-direction, altogether inimical to life in the religious state. They will never succeed in religious life, although they will be attracted to it and may live it for a time. I believe that many fallen-aways from the religious state are of this type. They did not have a right intention because they did not intend the necessary means to attain this common goal in the religious state.

The vocational director, therefore, should not prod, with a prejudiced eye, every nice boy into the priesthood and every nice girl into the religious state. God's ways are not our ways; and very often in vocational guidance we discover that our choice does not coincide with God's selection. Divine vocation to the supernatural organism of the Church demands a variety in the divine design.[81] God does extend a general invitation to the religious state. But for the greater good of the whole universe He influences some to enter this state of life and others to embrace other necessary states and occupations.[82] A vocational director must discern as best he can the divine effects influencing each individual response to the general invitation to religious life. The importance of a choice of state of life is much too important, affecting the eternal salvation of souls, for rash and precipitous judgment.

The religious state is not, as we have shown through St. Thomas, a state for the more perfect, but a state of perfection for all possessing the supernatural equipment of sanctifying grace and intent upon using the better means of religious life to attain the common Christian goal of perfection in charity. A director, therefore, should not delay an aspirant's entrance into religious life unnecessarily, awaiting probity of life through a faithful practice of the precepts. Nor should he merely give utterance to the general counsel of Christ and rush the aspirant into a fixed and solemn state of life. Again, a careful judgment, after a sufficient consideration of qualifications, must be made on the basis of available and manifested evidence.

The director ordinarily cannot perceive the inscrutable movement of the Holy Ghost. He cannot discern grace other than by its effects; for grace, like "the waters of Siloe, that go with silence" (Isaias, 8:16), is imperceptible, the gentle licking of an unseen Flame, the intangible touch of unheard Breath. The interior efficacy of divine operation may have the effect of almost conscious propulsion, fixing the subject in his or her inclination.[83] But even this extraordinary manifestation is difficult to discern and judge with certitude. Furthermore, such manifestations are extraordinary and rarely encountered.

The director must, as best he can, judge the subject's *propositum religionis.* He must discern a true intellectual consideration of the nature of the object of the aspirant's resolve, and recognize a firm resolve of the rational will. Some manifestation of the proper virtues effecting this resolve will be helpful. This is particularly true of magnanimity, which is assigned as the proper cause of the intensity required in the act of devotion essential to the religious resolve.

St. Thomas describes the qualities of a magnanimous person, and one can readily understand their need in religious life. He says that a magnanimous person will manifest a generosity of soul in his love of God and desire for virtue, social generosity in dealing with others, frankness and lack of pretense or deceit, moderation in accepting honors, a balanced appreciation of all God's creatures, and an absence of precipitous or presumptuous efforts.[84]

In encouraging and advising response to the invitation to religious life, the director should be mindful of the causes of devotion. Above all, charity "both causes devotion, inasmuch as love makes one prompt to serve one's friend, and is nourished by devotion."[85] Thus impelled by the love of God, the Christian soul will seek the total surrender of self to divine service. The extrinsic cause of devotion is meditation, especially on the humanity of Christ.[86] For the consideration of God's goodness enkindles love, which is the proximate cause of devotion. Therefore the practices of reciting the Rosary, following the Stations of the Cross, and the reading of the Gospels, will foster devotion. Attending the Holy Sacrifice of the Mass, especially assisting by way of serving or doing sacristy work, indicates a devotional readiness to serve God in the work of worship.

Impediments to devotion are all those things which debase man's mind, for without purity the mind cannot be applied to divine things. Hence the threefold cause of sin likewise effects loss of devotion and consequently loss of interest in religious life. Impurity, worldliness and pride, especially intellectual pride, are the enemies of God and of His household as well.[87]

As for the aspirant with good intentions, but

wavering in the resolve of will, Cardinal Cajetan recommends the following aids for stabilizing a firm and holy confidence in this decision and of acquiring the necessary *bona dispositio:* prayer, alms-giving, meditation, purification of conscience, the reading of Sacred Scripture and the hearing of sermons.

Much of the superficial fear of entering religion is unfounded and unreasonable. Often this fear is based on acquaintance with others who have tried religious life, failed and left. But, says St. Thomas, one might as well decide against embracing the faith because others have apostasized.[88] He compares such an attitude to those who would give up trying to be chaste because others are impure, or to a soldier quitting in battle because his buddies desert.[89]

St. Thomas often reminds us of the important "years of probation given to those entering, in which the difficulties of religion are tried."[90] Again, "those who are induced to enter religion still have a time of probation wherein they make a trial of the hardships of religion, so that they are not easily admitted to the religious life."[91] And so the director, after making a prudent judgment in advising an aspirant to try the religious state, should remember that he is not the final judge of the fitness of the subject before him.

The very purpose of the postulancy and novitiate in religious life is precisely to provide a mutual trial for the candidate and the institute.

Let St. Thomas Aquinas have the final words, conceived as they were in the wisdom and experience of a brilliant saint in the religious state:

The misgivings of those who hesitate as to whether or not they may be able to attain to perfection by entering religion is shown by many examples to be unreasonable . . .

To those who take this sweet yoke upon themselves He provides the refreshment of the divine fruition and the eternal rest of their souls.

To which may He who made this promise bring us, Jesus Christ, Our Lord, who is over all things blessed forever.

Amen

(St. Thomas Aquinas' final words of his *Contra Retrahentes*.)

NOTES

References to the works of St. Thomas Aquinas and commentators.

1. *Summa Theologica*, IIa-IIae, q. 186, q. 189
2. *Ibid.*, IIa-IIae, q. 189, a. 10
3. *Ibid.*, Ia-IIae, q. 108, a. 4
4. *Ibid.*, IIa-IIae, q. 88
5. *In Evangelium S. Matthaei Commentaria*, 19:12, 21
6. *Quaestiones Quodlibetales*, IV, q. 12, a. 1
7. *Summa Theologica*, Ia, q. 19, a. 11
8. *Ibid.*, Ia, q. 19, a. 12; Also *De Veritate*, q. 123, a. 3
9. *Summa Theologica*, Ia-IIae, q. 92, a. 2, ad 2um; Ia-IIae, q. 108, a. 4
10. *Ibid.*, Ia-IIae, q. 108, a. 4; *Summa Contra Gentiles*, lib. III, cap. 130
11. *Summa Theologica*, IIa-IIae, q. 184, a. 3; q. 189, a. 1, ad 3um; *Contra Gentiles*, lib. III, cap. 130; *Quodlibetales*, III, q. 12, a. 2; *De Perfectione Vitae Spiritualis*, cap. 1-6; *Contra Retrahentes*, cap. 6-7; Comm. in Matt., 19:21; In Epist. ad Hebr., 6:1
12. *Quodlibetales*, IV, q. 12, a. 2
13. *De Perfect. Vitae Spirit.*, cap. 6
14. *Quodlibetales*, IV, q. 12, a. 2
15. *Summa Theologica*, IIa-IIae, q. 186, a. 2
16. *Ibid.*, IIa-IIae, q. 186, a. 1, ad 4um; Ia, q. 9, a. 12, ad 4um
17. *Contra Retrahent.*, cap. 6
18. *Ibid.*, cap. 7
19. *Quodlibetales*, IV, q. 12, a. 1, ad 11um
20. *Summa Theologica*, IIa-IIae, q. 189, a. 9
21. *Ibid.*, IIa-IIae, q. 189, a. 10; in *Contra Retrahent.*, cap. 9 he speaks of those impeded "such as married people or slaves."

22. *Contra Retrahent.*, cap. 3-5
23. *Summa Theologica*, IIa-IIae, q. 186, a. 1, ad 4um
24. *Ibid.*, IIa-IIae, q. 189, a. 2-3
25. *Contra Retrahent.*, cap. 9-10
26. *Ibid.*, cap. 9
27. *Loc. cit.*
28. *Ibid.*
29. In Matt., cap. 19
30. In Matt., 19:11
31. In Matt., 19:11
32. In Matt., 19:11
33. *Contra Retrahent.*, cap. 9
34. In Epist. ad Rom., 8:30
35. In Matt., 4:19
36. *Ibid.*
37. *Contra Retrahent.*, cap. 10
38. *Loc. cit.*
39. *Ibid.*
40. *Contra Retrahent.*, cap. 10
41. *Contra Gent.*, I, 3
42. *Summa Theologica*, Ia-IIae, q. 108, a. 4, ad 1um
43. *Ibid.*, Ia-IIae, q. 106, a. 1, ad 1um
44. *Contra Retrahent.*, cap. 9
45. *Ortega, op. cit.*, p. 6
46. *Summa Theologica*, Ia, q. 103, a. 7
47. *Ibid.*, Ia, q. 23, a. 5
48. *Quodlibetales*, Iv, q. 12, a. 1, ad 8um
49. *Summa Theologica*, Ia, q. 19, a. 12, ad 3um
50. *Ibid.*, Ia-IIae, q. 90, prolog.
51. *Contra Retrahent.*, cap. 10
52. In Matt., 4:19
53. *Summa Theologica*, Ia-IIae, q. 112, a. 5
54. *Ortega, op. cit.*, p. 23
55. *Summa Theologica*, IIa-IIae, q. 81, a. 12
56. *Ibid.*, Ia, q. 22, a. 1
57. *Ibid.*, IIa-IIae, q. 86, a. 1. Also IIa-IIae, q. 186, a. 1, ad 2um; *Contra Gent.*, III, cap. 130
58. *Summa Theologica*, IIa-IIae, q. 88, a. 5
59. *Ibid.*, IIa-IIae, q. 81, a. 3-6

60. *Loc. cit.*, a. 6

61. *Ibid.*, IIa-IIae, q. 82, a. 1

62. *Ibid.*, IIa-IIae, q. 82, a. 1, ad 1um, a. 4, ad 1um, ad 2um

63. *Ibid.*, IIa-IIae, q. 82, a. 1, ad 1um

64. Garrigou-Lagrange, O.P., "De Speciali Inspiratione Spiritus Sancti Secundum Charitatis Augmentum," *Xenia Thomistica*, II, Romae, 1925, p. 223

65. *Summa Theologica*, IIa-IIae, q. 121, a. 1; Ia-IIae, q. 68, a. 4, ad 2um

66. *Ibid.*, IIa-IIae, q. 19

67. *Ibid.*, IIa-IIae, q. 139, a. 1

68. Walter Farrell, O.P., "Tranquil Violence," *Cross and Crown*, vol. 1, no. 3, p. 281

69. *Summa Theologica*, IIIa, q. 27, a. 4

70. *Ibid.*, IIa-IIae, q. 189, a. 9

71. *Ibid.*, IIa-IIae, q. 189, a. 10

72. *Contra Retrahent.*, cap. 9

73. *Summa Theologica*, Suppl., q. 41, a. 2, ad 4um. Also *Contra Gent.*, cap. 136

74. *Quodlibetales*, II, q. 4, a. 2

75. *Contra Retrahent.*, cap. 10

76. *Summa Theologica*, Ia, q. 19, a. 7

77. *Ibid.*, IIa-IIae, q. 189, a. 4, ad 3um

78. *Contra Retrahent.*, cap. 10; *Quodlibetales*, III, q. 5, a. 2

79. *Summa Theologica*, IIa-IIae, q. 189, a. 4, ad 1um

80. *De Perft. Vitae Spirit.*, cap. 6

81. In I Cor., 12:20

82. *Summa Theologica*, IIa-IIae, q. 183, a. 2

83. *Contra Retrahent.*, cap. 10

84. *Summa Theologica*, IIa-IIae, q. 129, a. 3, ad 3um, ad 5um, a. 4 ad 2um

85. *Ibid.*, IIa-IIae, q. 183, a. 3, ad 2um

86. *Ibid.*, IIa-IIae, q. 81, a. 8; q. 82, a. 3, ad 3um

87. *Contra Retrahent.*, cap. 10

88. In Matt., 19:11

89. *Quodlibetales*, III, q. 12, a. 1, ad 5um

90. *Summa Theologica*, IIa-IIae, q. 189, a. 9, ad 1um

If you have enjoyed this book, consider making your next selection from among the following . . .

Prices subject to change.

Prices subject to change.

Seven Capital Sins. *Benedictine Sisters* 3.00
Confession—Its Fruitful Practice. *Ben. Srs.* 3.00
Sermons of the Curé of Ars. *Vianney* 15.00
St. Antony of the Desert. *St. Athanasius* 7.00
Is It a Saint's Name? *Fr. William Dunne* 3.00
St. Pius V—His Life, Times, Miracles. *Anderson* 7.00
Who Is Therese Neumann? *Fr. Charles Carty.* 3.50
Martyrs of the Coliseum. *Fr. O'Reilly.* 21.00
Way of the Cross. *St. Alphonsus Liguori.* 1.50
Way of the Cross. *Franciscan version.* 1.50
How Christ Said the First Mass. *Fr. Meagher* 21.00
Too Busy for God? Think Again! *D'Angelo* 7.00
St. Bernadette Soubirous. *Trochu* 21.00
Pope Pius VII. *Anderson* 16.50
Treatise on the Love of God. 1 Vol. *de Sales. Mackey, Trans.* 27.50
Confession Quizzes. *Radio Replies Press* 2.50
St. Philip Neri. *Fr. V. J. Matthews.* 7.50
St. Louise de Marillac. *Sr. Vincent Regnault* 7.50
The Old World and America. *Rev. Philip Furlong.* 21.00
Prophecy for Today. *Edward Connor* 7.50
The Book of Infinite Love. *Mother de la Touche* 7.50
Chats with Converts. *Fr. M. D. Forrest.* 13.50
The Church Teaches. *Church Documents* 18.00
Conversation with Christ. *Peter T. Rohrbach* 12.50
Purgatory and Heaven. *J. P. Arendzen* 6.00
Liberalism Is a Sin. *Sarda y Salvany* 9.00
Spiritual Legacy of Sr. Mary of the Trinity. *van den Broek* 13.00
The Creator and the Creature. *Fr. Frederick Faber* 17.50
Radio Replies. 3 Vols. *Frs. Rumble and Carty* 48.00
Convert's Catechism of Catholic Doctrine. *Fr. Geiermann* 5.00
Incarnation, Birth, Infancy of Jesus Christ. *St. Alphonsus* 13.50
Light and Peace. *Fr. R. P. Quadrupani* 8.00
Dogmatic Canons & Decrees of Trent, Vat. I. *Documents* 11.00
The Evolution Hoax Exposed. *A. N. Field* 9.00
The Primitive Church. *Fr. D. I. Lanslots.* 12.50
The Priest, the Man of God. *St. Joseph Cafasso* 16.00
Blessed Sacrament. *Fr. Frederick Faber* 20.00
Christ Denied. *Fr. Paul Wickens* 3.50
New Regulations on Indulgences. *Fr. Winfrid Herbst* 3.00
A Tour of the Summa. *Msgr. Paul Glenn* 22.50
Latin Grammar. *Scanlon and Scanlon* 18.00
A Brief Life of Christ. *Fr. Rumble* 3.50
Marriage Quizzes. *Radio Replies Press* 2.50
True Church Quizzes. *Radio Replies Press.* 2.50
The Secret of the Rosary. *St. Louis De Montfort.* 5.00
Mary, Mother of the Church. *Church Documents* 5.00
The Sacred Heart and the Priesthood. *de la Touche* 10.00
Revelations of St. Bridget. *St. Bridget of Sweden* 4.50
Magnificent Prayers. *St. Bridget of Sweden* 2.00
The Happiness of Heaven. *Fr. J. Boudreau* 10.00
St. Catherine Labouré of the Miraculous Medal. *Dirvin* 16.50
The Glories of Mary. *St. Alphonsus Liguori* 21.00
Three Conversions/Spiritual Life. *Garrigou-Lagrange, O.P.* 7.00

Prices subject to change.

Spiritual Life. *Fr. Adolphe Tanquerey* 32.50
Freemasonry: Mankind's Hidden Enemy. *Bro. C. Madden* 8.00
Fourteen Holy Helpers. *Hammer* 7.50
All About the Angels. *Fr. Paul O'Sullivan* 7.50
AA-1025: Memoirs of an Anti-Apostle. *Marie Carré.* 7.50
All for Jesus. *Fr. Frederick Faber.* 16.50
Growth in Holiness. *Fr. Frederick Faber.* 18.00
Behind the Lodge Door. *Paul Fisher.* 21.00
Chief Truths of the Faith. (Book I). *Fr. John Laux* 12.50
Mass and the Sacraments. (Book II). *Fr. John Laux* 12.50
Catholic Morality. (Book III). *Fr. John Laux.* 12.50
Catholic Apologetics. (Book IV). *Fr. John Laux* 12.50
Introduction to the Bible. *Fr. John Laux* 18.00
Church History. *Fr. John Laux* 27.50
Devotion for the Dying. *Mother Mary Potter* 12.00
Devotion to the Sacred Heart. *Fr. Jean Croiset* 16.50
An Easy Way to Become a Saint. *Fr. Paul O'Sullivan.* 7.00
The Golden Arrow. *Sr. Mary of St. Peter.* 15.00
The Holy Man of Tours. *Dorothy Scallan.* 15.00
Hell—Plus How to Avoid Hell. *Fr. Schouppe/Nelson* 15.00
History of Protestant Ref. in England & Ireland. *Cobbett* 21.00
Holy Will of God. *Fr. Leo Pyzalski.* 7.50
How Christ Changed the World. *Msgr. Luigi Civardi* 9.00
How to Be Happy, How to Be Holy. *Fr. Paul O'Sullivan* 9.00
Imitation of Christ. *Thomas à Kempis. (Challoner transl.)* 15.00
Life & Message of Sr. Mary of the Trinity. *Rev. Dubois* 12.00
Life Everlasting. *Fr. Garrigou-Lagrange, O.P.* 16.50
Life of Mary as Seen by the Mystics. *Compiled by Raphael Brown* 15.00
Life of St. Dominic. *Mother Augusta Drane* 15.00
Life of St. Francis of Assisi. *St. Bonaventure* 12.50
Life of St. Ignatius Loyola. *Fr. Genelli* 18.50
Life of St. Margaret Mary Alacoque. *Rt. Rev. Emile Bougaud* 15.00
Mexican Martyrdom. *Fr. Wilfrid Parsons* 12.50
Children of Fatima. *Windeatt. (Age 10 & up)* 11.00
Cure of Ars. *Windeatt. (Age 10 & up)* 13.00
The Little Flower. *Windeatt. (Age 10 & up)* 11.00
Patron of First Communicants. (Bl. Imelda). *Windeatt. (Age 10 & up)* 8.00
Miraculous Medal. *Windeatt. (Age 10 & up)* 9.00
St. Louis De Montfort. *Windeatt. (Age 10 & up)* 13.00
St. Thomas Aquinas. *Windeatt. (Age 10 & up)* 8.00
St. Catherine of Siena. *Windeatt. (Age 10 & up)* 7.00
St. Rose of Lima. *Windeatt. (Age 10 & up)* 10.00
St. Hyacinth of Poland. *Windeatt. (Age 10 & up)* 13.00
St. Martin de Porres. *Windeatt. (Age 10 & up)* 10.00
Pauline Jaricot. *Windeatt. (Age 10 & up)* 15.00
Douay-Rheims New Testament. *Paperbound* 16.50
Prayers and Heavenly Promises. *Compiled by Joan Carroll Cruz* 6.00
Preparation for Death. (Unabr., pocket). *St. Alphonsus* 13.50
Rebuilding a Lost Faith. *John Stoddard* 16.50
The Spiritual Combat. *Dom Lorenzo Scupoli* 12.00
Retreat Companion for Priests. *Fr. Francis Havey* 9.00
Spiritual Doctrine of St. Cath. of Genoa. *Marabotto/St. Catherine* 12.50
The Soul of the Apostolate. *Dom Chautard* 12.50

Prices subject to change.

At your Bookdealer or direct from the Publisher.

Toll-Free 1-800-437-5876   *Fax 815-226-7770*
Tel. 815-226-7777   ***www.tanbooks.com***

Prices subject to change.

FR. RICHARD BUTLER, O.P.
1918-1988

One of six children, Fr. Richard Butler was born in Salem, Massachusetts in 1918. He attended prep schools before going on to undergraduate studies at Notre Dame University and the Catholic University of America. Upon entering the Dominican Order in 1942, the author studied philosophy and theology at the Domincan House of Studies in River Forest, Illinois. He was ordained in 1949. That year, Father Butler began two years of study at the Angelicum in Rome, where he received his doctorate in philosophy in 1952.

Fr. Butler's most active years were spent in teaching and campus ministry, particularly through various Newman Centers; from 1962-1964 he served as National Chaplain of the Newman Apostolate. In 1974-1975, during a "sabbatical," he taught at the University of Dallas' Rome campus. Fr. Butler received numerous awards over the years, including the Notre Dame Man of the Year award.

In 1965 Fr. Butler had been appointed consultor to the Vatican's Secretariat for Unbelievers. In 1976, in response to a growing need, Fr. Butler undertook to oversee the revision and republication of the Dominican Order's *Challenge of Christ* high school religion series.

Vocational work was always of great interest to Father, and he wrote material for his order on this subject, as well as making a special study of vocational theology. A regular speaker on college campuses, as well as a contributor to several magazines, including *Commonweal* and *The Critic*, Father Butler also authored *The Mind of Santayana* (Regnery, 1955) and *The Life and World of George Santayana* (Regnery, 1960). In these books he explored the thought of this baptized "confused skeptic" whom he had known as a personal friend. Santayana had spent his life standing "at the church door"—an agnostic situation which Fr. Butler felt was shared by many 20th-century men. In Fr. Butler's last book, *Witness to Change: A Cultural Memoir*, he recounted and offered a critical analysis of developments that he had seen in the Church and in society during the years from 1925 to 1975.

Fr. Butler went to his reward in 1988 after suffering a cardiac arrest while visiting his family in Massachusetts. His grave is located in the Dominican plot at All Saints Cemetery, Des Plaines, Illinois.